THE ENERGY OF RECEIVING

Happy Publishing

The Energy of Receiving

Compiled and Edited by Erica Glessing

FIRST EDITION

ISBN 978-0-9895554-9-4

Cover Design by Melinda Asztalos

Interior Design & Typography by
www.BookPublishingMentor.com

Published by Happy Publishing, www.HappyPublishing.net

Happy Publishing

The Energy of Receiving

"The energy of receiving is our innate ability to line dance with the universe. The planet receives from the sun, the grass receives from the rain, the baby receives nourishment from the mother. Most of us are weary, rusty, and our shoes are all wrong, but all we have to do is show up, get in line and let the music of creation make us nimble."

– Cherie Lawrence, RealYouNow.com

Table of Contents

Chapter 1

The Golden Heart Cycle of Creation: Allowing the Energy of Receiving to Flow

By Sylvie Olivier

I am so excited to share The Golden Heart Cycle of Creation with you. This Cycle of Creation represents the exact process of receiving my inspirations and intuitions and how they end up, fully manifested in a very concrete way. I play with this Cycle of Creation in my life every single day and I'm about to share it with you so that YOU too can play with it and start manifesting the life you are here to live!

Welcome to the Golden Heart Cycle of Creation!

As human beings, it is our very nature to create. We are Pure Creator Consciousness residing in a physical body. Accessing a high vibrational frequency assists us in the dissolution of old patterns and crystallized emotions that block us from experiencing and fully expressing our magnificence. These patterns are formed by beliefs and mental archives located at the base of the skull, while crystallized emotions are mainly located in the glandular and nervous systems. By becoming aware of this fact, and by dissolving patterns and crystallized emotions, it is much easier to let Creation manifest itself through us. We receive ideas and inspirations with clarity, as they are no longer filtered by mass consciousness or by our own programs. This unveiled clarity assists us in co-creating with the Universe by taking inspired actions. As Pure Creator Consciousness, we let the Cycle of Creation manifest itself through us, with grace and ease. Without a single shortcut, we allow ourselves to be loved, cherished, nurtured, honored and taken care of with the best of the best that the Universe has to offer, in every situation! Now, how do we do that? Simply.

Introducing The Golden Heart Cycle of Creation

The Golden Heart Cycle of Creation goes beyond a shift in paradigm; it's a completely new paradigm; a 180-degree move in the opposite direction from what most people believe in. The Cycle of Creation, when able to flow freely without its walls, will put an end to the endless quest of always needing to look outside of YOURSELF for answers.

When I first received the inspiration for The Cycle of Creation, it was split into four chambers of Golden Heart in four distinct quadrants.

Cycle of Creation

by Golden Heart Wisdom

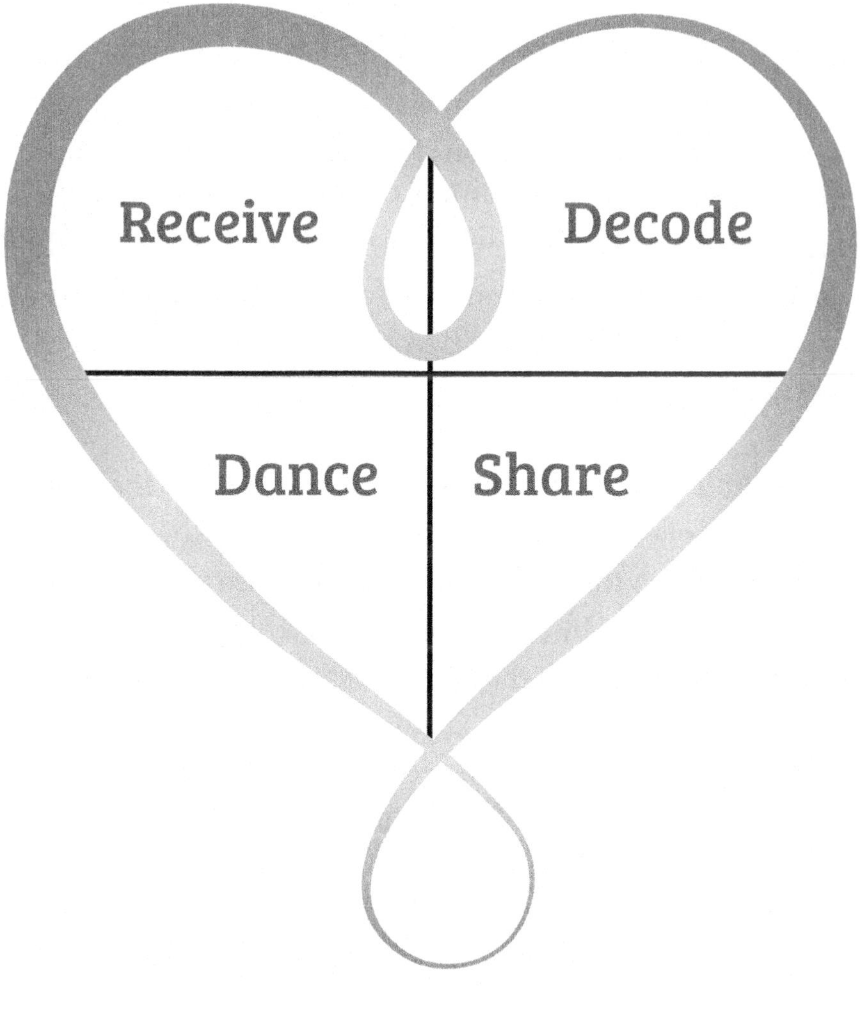

The Universe shared its wisdom with me by sending me the awareness, the words and the illustration to effectively communicate this concept.

When I receive an inspiration, it always arrives the same way, almost like a download. The best way I can explain it is as follows: Imagine the inside of a golf ball, consisting of hundreds of elastic type bands knitted and bound tightly together. Then I decode the inspiration. I become aware of the inspiration, of what Creation is birthing through me. The elastic bands then unravel into one endless string and are now in a state of completion. Then it comes time to share the beautiful inspiration with the world, whether it is with my husband, my family, my team, my clients or the world. Finally, we dance the inspiration, meaning that we experience this particular inspiration in our three dimensional world!!!

I now use The Cycle of Creation with my clients so they can clearly see where their resistances lie and where the ego tries to keep them in the status quo. Once they are aware of the resistances formed by beliefs, patterns and old programs, it's much easier for them to choose to release them. This therefore increases their vibrational frequency and they are free to be in a state of expansion while they co-create with the Universe. Let's take a look at the four quadrants of The Cycle of Creation.

1. Receive (seeding): The Receive quadrant represents our ability to be open and receive inspirations, ideas, resources and intuitions. Some people see images, others hear words

Cycle of Creation

by Golden Heart Wisdom

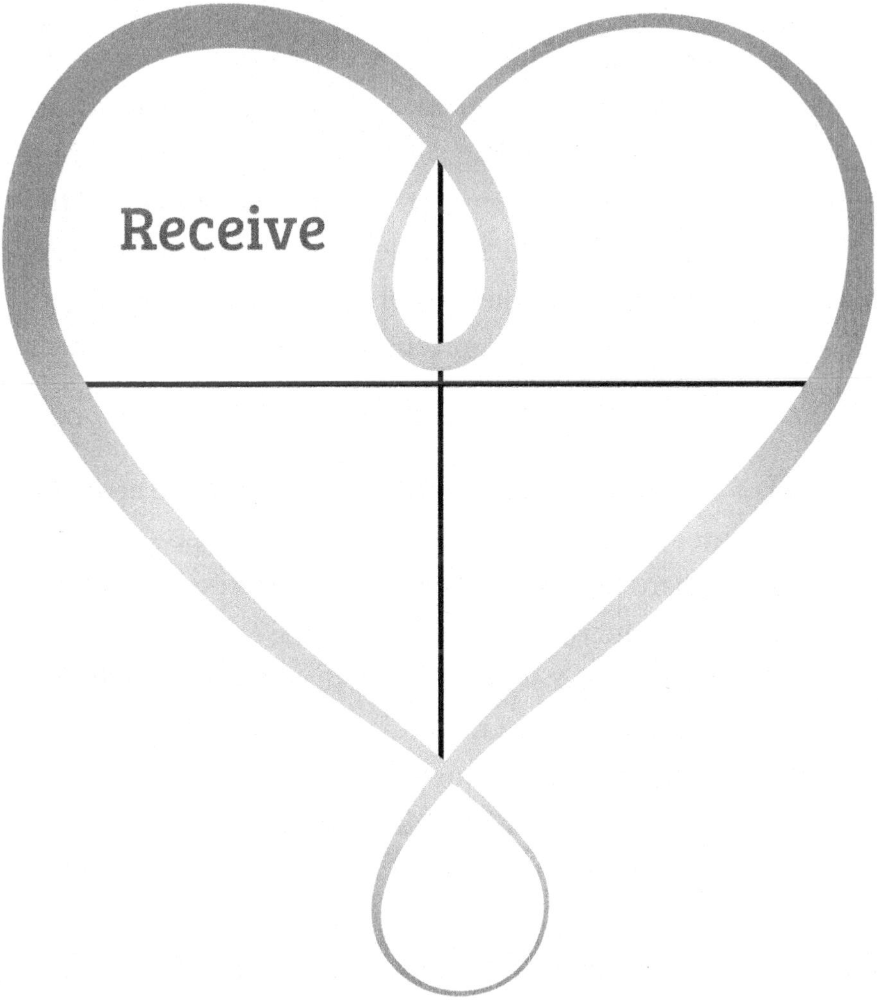

while others like me, feel. They are all perfect forms and not one of them is better than the other. It's simply a matter of practice. Practicing the gift of Receiving will enable you to live through The Cycle of Creation, where every area of your personal and professional life can unfold to its highest potential. The key element here is to live in what I call Welcoming Mode, where you're free of all beliefs, opinions and judgments that limit you as Pure Creator Consciousness.

In the many years where I assisted people, I have yet to meet someone who's never received inspirations or ideas; we all do. However, what we do with them depends on many factors: belief systems, judgments, memories and the cultural structure in which we were raised. When we allow ourselves to RECEIVE the gifts of inspiration and intuition, we manifest all kinds of graceful and magical experiences into our lives!

Most of us learned to disconnect from our Essence at a very young age. We were taught to improve ourselves and to work very hard to succeed. This learning process masked the perfection of who we are as our Divine Essence and instilled within many of us a sense of brokenness and inadequacy; putting us on a path to never ending self-improvement. Little by little, we closed ourselves off from receiving and gradually, we stopped seeing, listening and feeling the voice of our intuition.

The Receive quadrant represents the seeding stage. When

we put a seed in the soil in the appropriate environment, we know that it will germinate, emerge and finally blossom to its full capacity.

The same process applies with us. When we receive the seed of inspiration and allow it to bathe in the proper environment, which is a high vibrational frequency, inspiration will then follow the next steps of The Cycle of Creation. This high vibrational frequency is actually the natural state of our Divine Essence.

Expanding Your Awareness of the Receive Quadrant

Stop and take a moment right now to remember times when you knew deep down that you were receiving inspirations and intuitions. Did you follow their voice or did you go about your day and not pay attention?

When you followed their voice, how did you feel? Bring awareness to the energy that came with your choice. Feel it and breathe into it. How does it feel? Does it feel expansive, energizing and allowing?

When you ignored the voice, how did you feel? Bring awareness to the energy that came with your choice. Feel it and breathe into it. How does it feel? Does it feel constrictive, exhausting and stressful?

Now take a moment, breathe and open yourself up to receiving. Your breath along with this new awareness will activate the seed for receiving in your life, with grace and with ease. Bring awareness to the energy that lies behind the emotion of receiving, and create space to allow for all of the gifts the Universe has in store for you. This energy will enrich the seeding process. As you allow yourself to receive with clarity; your vibration raises while you watch the magic of life flow into your experience. You open yourself up to exponential receiving. You connect with your unique gift that the world is waiting for you to fully express; creating the perfect environment for the next step in The Cycle of Creation: the Decode quadrant which is where germination occurs.

2. Decode (germinating). The Decode quadrant represents our ability to become aware of what Creation is birthing through us, without trying, and without goal-oriented efforts. When we allow ourselves to go beyond the mind, we connect with our Essence on a deeper level and we open the doors to the universal libraries, thus accessing Divinity's omnipotence and omnipresence. These universal libraries contain the purest and highest form of universal information and data. Access to these universal libraries is available to all of us once we've released old patterns and truly connected with our Divinity. We are then open and able to be the architect of an entirely new blueprint for our creation. What's most important here is to NOT let our mind or focus interfere since we do not need to plan every single detail for our inspiration to manifest itself. This is the time to let go of the reins and let LIFE work for us! This is that Ah ha moment! Our own Eureka!!!

Cycle of Creation

by Golden Heart Wisdom

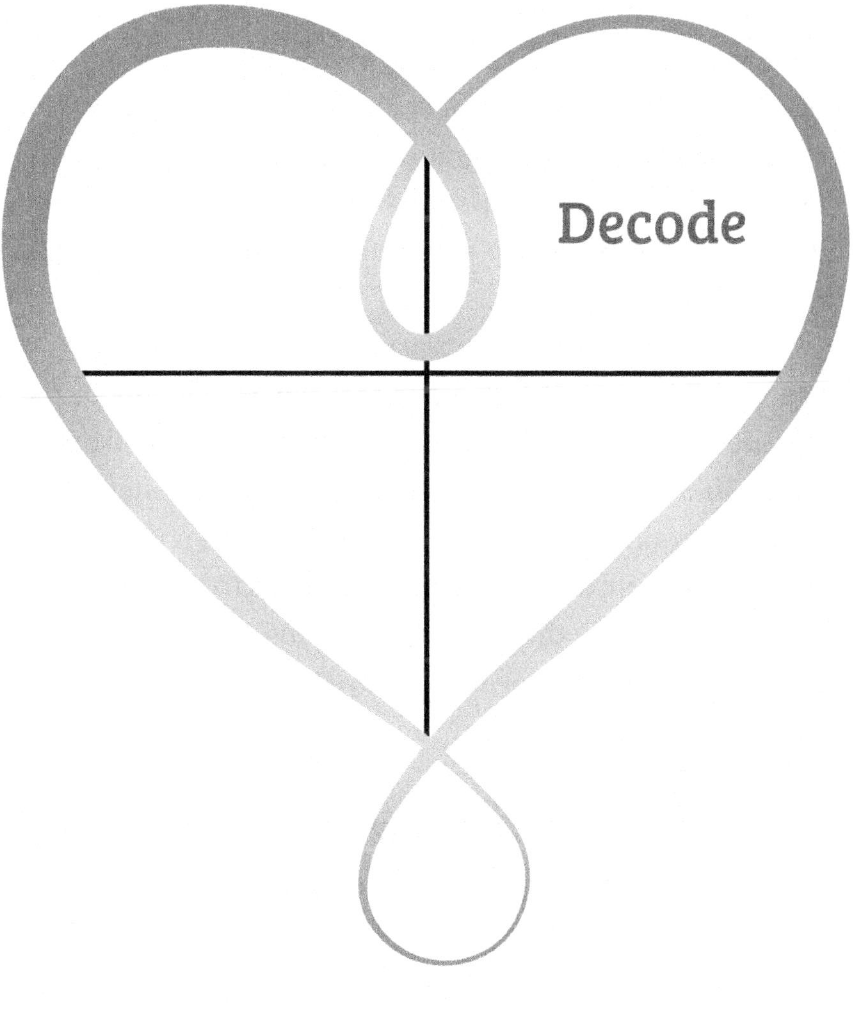

Many people stop here because of past programming that tells us we need to be in a *Searching Mode* rather than a *Welcoming Mode.* When we're in *Searching Mode,* we have to make things happen. We've been trained to think it's the only way to survive and thrive. It is therefore natural that this be our first impulse reaction. We were taught that in order to achieve our goals, we had to work hard. How many times did we hear: *'if you want something in life, you have to roll up your sleeves and work hard to get it'*? Or maybe an inspiration came through you and you thought you didn't have the necessary resources to manifest it: money, time, people! When we put breaks on our inspiration because we think we have too many obstacles, we prevent ourselves from living the life of our dreams AND we prevent humanity from fully enjoying our unique gift!

We were also raised to believe that we are victims of the outside world and reality; that our current reality will determine our success or failure. This whole belief system is so deeply ingrained in society that it created an endless loop in which we run, always waiting for things to change before we can finally live the life of our dreams. There's always a perfect excuse for why we can't move forward with our most heartfelt inspirations.

The Decode quadrant represents the germination stage. Once in the proper environment; the seed will begin the growth process through germination and thus prepare itself to emerge.

In the Decode quadrant, most people try to attract something from the outside, not fully aware that it all begins in your own awareness, in your consciousness; not in your capacity to cleverly attract the object of your desire. When you believe that you need to attract from the outside, you are living in scarcity and lack and that is the message you're sending out. The Universe is expansive and will take your energetic signal and give it expansion. So by sending a lack signal into the Universe, guess what... you'll receive MORE lack and it will expand exponentially.

The Law of Attraction finds its roots in polarity and duality. The beauty of "The Golden Heart Cycle of Creation" is that you connect with neutrality instead of living in duality (polarity). In neutrality, the Decode quadrant is activated without the intervention of the ego/mind and polarity. You are no longer trapped and you can go beyond the electromagnetic field of the Law of Attraction. You don't need to fight it... you simply outgrow it!

Everything that comes into your life MUST first germinate in your consciousness.

In the Decode quadrant, all of the necessary conditions for you to be able to share your inspiration will be met. You will be inspired to take specific actions, if it requires others to take specific actions; they will be inspired to do so without being in Searching Mode! By being connected to your Divine Essence, the reality that you are living in right now will reorganize itself to match your high vibration! You will therefore be aware of what Creation is birthing through you and you'll become the co-creative partner of your new reality.

Expanding Your Awareness of the Decode Quadrant

Stop and take a moment right now to quiet your mind and be still. Remember an instance where you received an inspiration and you started to feel excited about it, but for some reason, you were distracted and forgot or purposely set it aside. Feel the emotions that are coming up and breathe. This will activate the process of dissolving their crystallizations in your body.

Now, ask yourself why you're struggling to manifest this inspiration. Are you stuck in Searching Mode, having to make things happen? Do you feel like a victim of conditions, people or society?

• Are you waiting for people to show up and to change their behavior?

• Are you waiting for the right timing or for money before you can allow yourself to move forward?

• Are you waiting to get healthier or to be able to perform better?

If you're stuck in this quadrant, you are not living your life to the fullest. You are not letting the seed of your inspiration germinate and you are still waiting for that perfect timing or for something or someone to change, whether it is YOU or someone else.

Good news! This is not how The Cycle of Creation works! Creation and manifestation don't happen to you, they happen through you. It's so much easier than what you might think! By unveiling Pure Creator Consciousness and by letting it expand exponentially, you naturally become aware of the wonders that Creation is manifesting through you; as you watch the seed of your inspiration germinate. What's of utmost importance here is that you see that ***you ARE fulfilled right now****, without lacking or feeling limited or letting the outside world affect you.*

Now take a moment to breathe to be open to Decode, not in order to make anything happen, but as Pure Creator Consciousness. Ask your Divine Essence to show you the way, to guide you and inspire you regarding the actions that you have to take. This new awareness will activate the germination of the energy of decoding in your life, with grace and ease. Feel the emotion of decoding this wonderful inspiration that you received. Your consciousness will fertilize the germination process. And as you allow yourself to become aware of what Creation is birthing through you, your vibration will continue to rise as you watch the magic of life flow into your experience. You open the doors to the universal libraries, accessing all necessary resources to manifest your inspiration therefore creating the perfect environment for the next step of The Cycle of Creation: the Share quadrant which is where your inspiration emerges and becomes visible in your Reality.

3. Share (emerging). The Share quadrant represents our inspiration that is becoming visible for the first time in our three dimensional world. This is when we share our inspiration with at least one other person. We received an inspiration, an idea or an intuition and then we decoded it, meaning that we became aware of what Creation made available to us. This quadrant is both very exciting and scary all at the same time. So many questions usually pop in our minds: "What if I don't succeed!" or "What if I'm rejected or humiliated?" "What if this? What if that? What if? What if?" The ego/mind will try to avoid, repress, push away or hide anything that will put its existence in jeopardy! At this point, the ego gets trickier and will find ways to distract you or make you believe that this inspiration is not a good idea after all. It will tell you that dancing with The Cycle of Creation can be dangerous since it is time to let your divine inspiration emerge, thus becoming visible and known by the outside world!

Connecting with our Divine Essence is crucial; the deep knowing of our wholeness and completeness activates our willingness to share our unique gift with the world. The ego/mind is always afraid to die and wants to protect the part of us that needs labels and titles such as name, status, and career and so on, at all cost. This isn't something evil that we need to fight; rather, we can enjoy living with these attributes without letting them define who we are. We are not our name, our culture, or our gender. We are Pure Creator Consciousness having a beautiful experience in a physical body.

By opening yourself up to the process of Receive, Decode and now Share, you let the Universe take care of all the details.

Cycle of Creation

by Golden Heart Wisdom

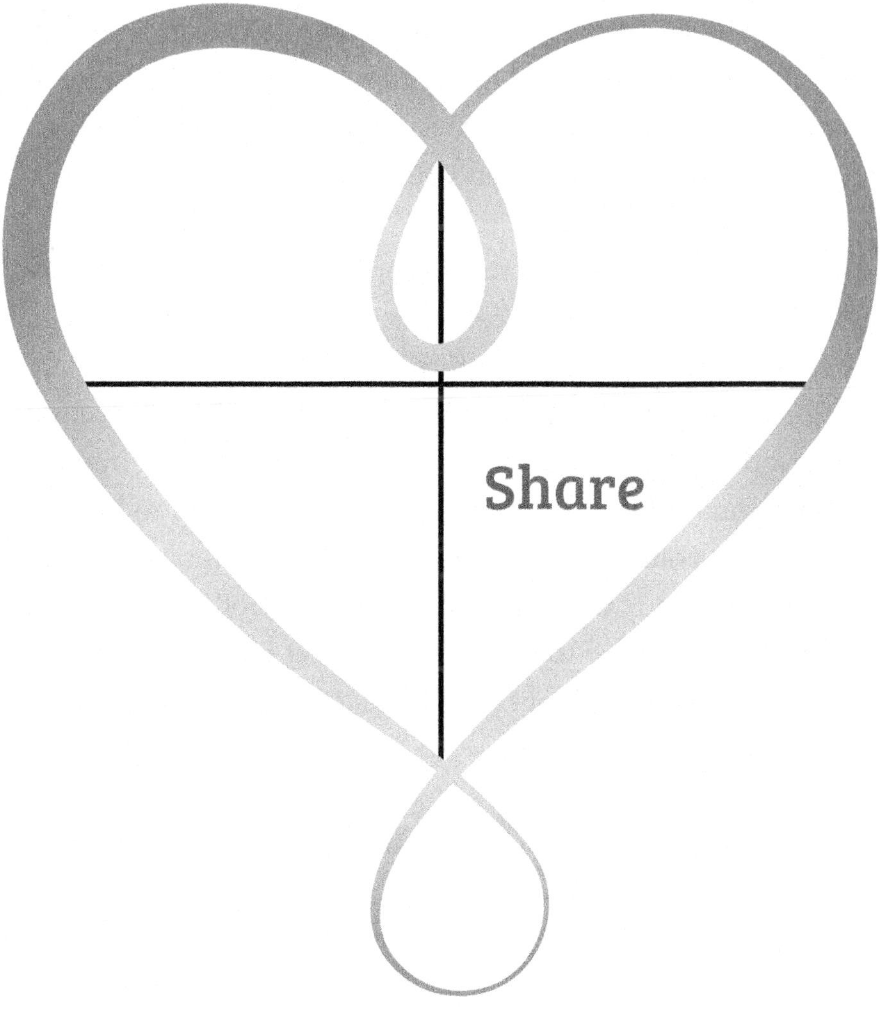

You let LIFE work for you and through you. This declaration may seem too good to be true and completely out of reach. But it works! I invite you to have your own experience before dismissing this Truth.

Most of us have been raised in polarity and duality where everyone has their own truths and perceptions. This concept of duality has created so many disagreements, conflicts and wars. The Truth that I'm referring to is not my truth; it is THE TRUTH for every single human being. This Truth resides in neutrality and is more than ready to emerge now! Will you accept it and welcome it in your life?

Allowing this Truth to emerge connects us to our full potential. This quadrant may seem tricky at first because when you share your inspiration with the world, you're opening up to its manifestation potential. Following a short transition period, it will become visible. Just prior to jumping into the Share quadrant, inspiration is invisible, waiting to be activated by your willingness to say your big vibrational YES and being ready to release the need for control! The more you try and work hard to focus on what you want to see, touch, hear, and feel, the longer it will take for your inspiration to manifest and be tangible.

The sharing quadrant represents the stage of emergence. This is when germination is over, and the seed is now ready to emerge and be seen.

Old models of science have tinted our creativity and awareness, making us believe that duality and separation are the ultimate reality. With the insights and wisdom now available, it's now known that duality isn't our true nature. We are living in a field of infinite possibilities, waiting to let our Pure Creator Consciousness emerge and take command.

Expanding Your Awareness of the Share Quadrant

Now take a moment to just BE and breathe. Inhale and exhale slowly and let your breathing expand to your whole being, filling every cell of your body. Allow your consciousness to open, let it present you with a time when you were so excited to share a great idea with someone. It may be with your spouse, your parents, your children, your friend or even a work colleague. Let yourself relive the experience of it now. How did you feel just before sharing your inspiration?

Now that you've shared your experience…remember how were you received? Was it with openness, joy, and encouragement? Or was it with judgment, insignificance and derision? You probably experienced both in your life.

Let's start by when you were ridiculed…how did you feel? Let yourself truly feel the different emotions coming up, and breathe. Allow them to dissolve and become sensations instead of crystallized emotions. Let them be FREE as you free yourself from these old patterns of beliefs, and the pain. Breathe and allow… breathe and allow… breathe and allow. Remember that these emotions are your perceptions of a truth; whether it was yours or someone else's. This is not who you are!

Now, let's bring an experience when you were received with openness, joy and encouragement. How did you feel? Can you feel the tingling inside? This is the energy that is bringing all the particles of consciousness into molecules to manifest in a visible way, just in front of you! This is YOU experiencing the true nature of being Pure Creator Consciousness.

Be aware that ***you don't need approval*** *from anyone to let Creation manifest itself through you. How others perceive you or do not perceive you does not matter. We tend to wait for people to take sides, be on our side, but do you see how polarized that is when we give power to one side or the other? When you free yourself from the outside world and all the beliefs, judgments, opinions and memories, the Share quadrant will flow easily, bringing your full potential into the last quadrant, the Dance quadrant where you will experience the full blossoming of your inspiration.*

4. Dance (blossoming). The Dance quadrant represents the complete manifestation of our inspiration in our three dimensional world. It is the last quadrant of The Cycle of Creation and this is when we fully enjoy the concrete manifestation of our inspiration. We are dancing hand in hand with all the resources that the Universe has in store for us. You expose the expression of your creativity; whether it is a book that you wrote and is now in your hands and available to the world; or a product that you created to assist humanity; or a party that you organized to celebrate a significant event. It doesn't matter what it is, since you totally allowed Creation to manifest itself through you. This is dancing time!

Cycle of Creation

by Golden Heart Wisdom

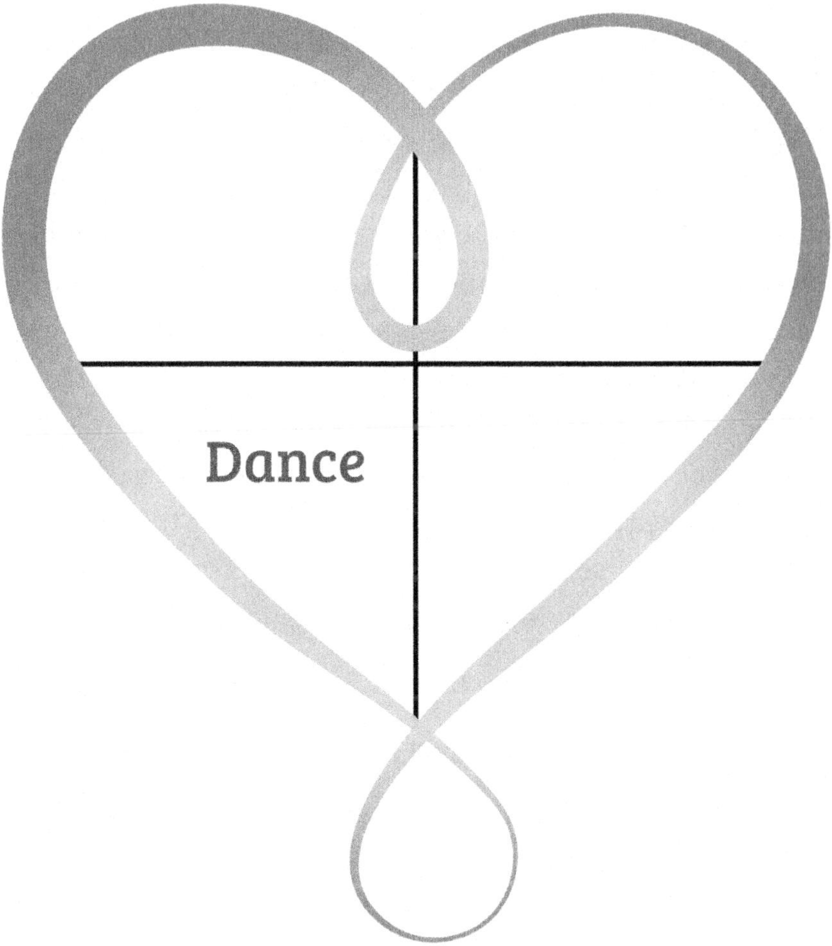

The Dance quadrant represents the full blossoming of the seed that was planted in the invisible realm of consciousness where divine inspiration exists in the first place. It represents the manifestation of your inspiration's blueprint and the full blossoming of the oak after its emergence from the acorn. This quadrant represents the wonder of Creation fully manifested.

In order for this quadrant to blossom, it is vital to be aware of patterns that are still running and acting as weeds and toxic elements preventing the seed from germinating, emerging and then blossoming. As you become conscious of the thoughts that you had as beliefs, you free yourself. Thoughts are live deities and surround us like a sea of thinking matter. Most of us spend a lot of time in our head, so without being aware of it, we allow thoughts to come in and we buy into them, adding to the beliefs already present in the mental archives at the base of the skull. So the same process begins again and again and again. Thoughts are not the Truth… they have been selected and "brought in" by other people and we tend to buy into them, thinking that they are accurate.

The more you become aware of the thoughts that you accepted as beliefs, the easier it will be to come to terms with them. And once you are willing to stop holding on to these beliefs, they will dissolve and you will access the universal libraries.

Some of us accepted the beliefs that we were unlovable,

unworthy or undeserving. By allowing ourselves to feel the emotions that are linked to these patterns, we free ourselves. Isn't that amazing? We don't have to get rid of them by trying or working hard, we free ourselves by allowing and breathing into the feelings!

If we believe that we are not good enough, we will sabotage this quadrant. Up until now, we received the seed of a wonderful inspiration and we decoded it by becoming aware of what Creation was birthing through us during the germination process.

We then shared our inspiration with someone else as we let it emerge and become visible. And now, in order to allow the full blossoming of our inspiration, we have to release the patterns of being unlovable, unworthy or undeserving... by doing so, the fabric of Pure Love that we are made of will automatically blossom and the life of our dreams will manifest itself before our very own eyes.

This is the Truth in neutrality. Knowing that we are loved, cherished and nurtured and honored beyond measure IS the basis of The Golden Heart Cycle of Creation!

Pure love, abundance, beauty, harmony, playfulness, lightness, laughter, joy, freedom and bliss are attributes of Divinity. They are at the core of The Cycle of Creation and complete the full circle! This is when all of the walls between each quadrant collapse and are dissolved.

Expanding Your Awareness of the Dance Quadrant

Whenever you have a moment, take some time to write down some of the beliefs that you've accepted along the way about being unlovable or unworthy or undeserving. Allow the memories to surface and then, breathe. The simple act of breathing while you feel these emotions will dissolve them. You don't have to try or work hard in order to dissolve… in fact; you cannot do it with your will. That's impossible. Just breathe and allow… breathe and allow… breathe and allow.

I invite you to welcome Pure Love… love is not a fancy feeling. Pure Love is the fabric that you are made of. This is who you are at your core!

Gently bring your attention to the top of your head… inside your head and feel, see or imagine a beautiful wave of Golden Light starting to move through your head, going down and relaxing every part of your head… This beautiful wave of Golden Light continues its way down into your neck… feel all tension going away… melting away.
Keep breathing and see, feel or imagine the wave of Golden Light going through your shoulders, your chest and through your abdomen and in your belly as if you were receiving a massage from the inside. Feel the sensation of being released from any stress and tension… the wave is moving into your arms and down into your legs.

Take a deep breath and feel the energy moving with fluidity and grace.

Your whole body is now relaxed... free of any tension or stress. The wave is now becoming a beautiful spiral of Golden Light moving from the top of your head to the tips of your fingers... and to the tips of your toes. It is like the sun, warm and somehow fluid like a quiet waterfall gliding from a golden river... It pours in you in a kind of fountain of youth and Pure Love.

Prepare yourself to Dance with all opportunities life presents as you reap a bountiful harvest.

Conclusion

Many luminaries and artists over the centuries experienced the fluidity and grace of The Cycle of Creation. When you deeply connect to your Divine Essence and you bathe in this universal space of Pure Love that many called unified field, you are loved, cherished, nurtured, honored and taken care of with the best of the best... the Universe is taking no shortcuts to present you with the highest opportunities to assist you and humanity! You can now relax into this Truth and allow peace to surround you and move through you.

YOU ARE LOVE and YOU ARE LOVED beyond your wildest imagination!

When you play with The Golden Heart Cycle of Creation, you stop struggling and trying to make things happen. You stop working hard on yourself to become a better person or to learn something else before you get there! Your Divine Essence unveils your true nature with grace and ease; and you live from your highest potential. You welcome Pure Love, joy, wonder, abundance in all its forms, a plethora of divine opportunities and enriching relationships.

You LIVE to the fullest!

Be kind to yourself as you would be for your best friend or your child! There is absolutely no guilt or blame that will live in the universal space of Pure Love that you are, as long as YOU allow it!

I hold you in a very sacred space… in my Golden Heart!

Much love,
Sylvie

ABOUT THE AUTHOR: *SYLVIE OLIVIER*

Sylvie Olivier, Master Alchemist and Energy Expert, brings magic into people's lives by sharing Golden Heart's Wisdom. Energy and alchemy have always fascinated her and at the age of five, she remembers flicking her wrist and wondering why the apple she desired wasn't already in her hand. She had already begun connecting with her wonderful gift of alchemy.

At the age of twenty, while expecting her

Cycle of Creation

by Golden Heart Wisdom

first child, she experienced the sudden loss of her mother, which caused an extremely violent emotional shock. That day marked the start of the creation of her armor which she built to keep pain away, never quite allowing her emotions to surface from fear of suffering even more. This pivotal moment marked the beginning of her own awakening.

Years later, the floor collapsed from under her. Her husband filed for divorce to pursue his life with her best friend, who also happened to be her sister in law. Then, her young daughter became so ill that death was the only feasible option if a rapid blood transfusion wasn't done quickly. With only her two daughters, she watched her world collapse as she lost her home, her husband, her money and her life.

Old sufferings resurfaced to guide her to change her perspective. She shifted her mindset to one of receiving and saw this series of events as a gift towards her discovery of the Essence of Gratitude. Gradually, gratitude literally transformed her life. Her book *Gratitude in Action ∞ Actions of Gratitude* gives a detailed rendition of her journey and offers tools and insights that assisted her in seeing the light in her darkest hour. That is when miracles began emerging in all spheres of her life. She became open to receiving what the universe had in store for her as she was more and more connected with her heart. She welcomed everything that showed up in her life without giving it a positive or negative label, she simply welcomed all of it.

Today, Sylvie Olivier is living in pure joy as she lives in harmony with her life purpose. That purpose is to be in alignment with her Divine Essence, the divine truth of who she really is; and she lets it shine for the world. Surrounded by her two very healthy adult daughters, she is now a loving grandmother. Happily remarried for over nineteen years to a wonderful man who's been a true blessing in her life; she shares how her experience with her ex-husband was a blessing as it led her to learn how to shift into a state of reception. He certainly played a pivotal role in her awakening and it needed to happen exactly as it did in order to lead her to reawaken to her true Essence. She is letting abundance in all its forms flow easily and gracefully into her life.

Today, Sylvie assists people in connecting with their true Essence, their own unique gifts and purpose to truly express their authentic divine selves. Once they are able to connect with their pure Essence, they can then be in a position of reception. Rather than working hard and trying to force things in a certain direction, the direction that our ego wants us to take. Sylvie shares how much simpler it is to be in a state of receiving.

When we are connected to our Divine Essence and are willing and ready to simply greet, opportunities for abundance, love and happiness will simply show up. Being in a receiving mode allows us to live with grace and ease. This assists us in dissolving crystallized emotions to truly connect with our heart, even in the midst of crises and chaos.

Through her signature process, Sylvie activates people's Golden Hearts, the most direct doorway to their Divine Essence, a sacred space inside each of us, where everything is possible. This space of high energetic vibrational frequency transmutes ancient beliefs and patterns, fears, heaviness and emotions (what she calls Lead Consciousness) into profound joy and the free expression of our Highest Self, our divine Essence (what she calls Gold Consciousness).

In Gold Consciousness, our heart opens to the divinity of our Essence. Our body aligns with its innate intelligence. In this state of consciousness, we do not have to do anything, we are simply who we are and are ready and open to dance with the opportunities that the universe presents us. It is phenomenal how a few inspired actions produce extraordinary results when we welcome our intuitions, opportunities, resources and ideas, rather than searching for them.

For many years, people asked Sylvie how she was able to create so many great things in such a small amount of time and she was never able to give them a proper answer, until now. She recently received the inspiration to create the Golden Heart Cycle of Creation, which is a wonderful tool that perfectly represents her process of receiving inspiration and intuition and how they end up, fully manifested in her life.

In addition to Sylvie's expansive life experiences of connecting with her own Divine Essence and living the life she is meant for, she also studied Bioenergetics for more than 7 years at the Alternative Medicine College of Canada. For over ten years, Sylvie was a well-known health adviser and teacher as she continued to learn a multitude of modalities such as quantum physics and sacred geometry, always wanting to enrich her practice. She's also a certified practitioner of the Emotional Freedom Technique (EFT) as well as of The One Command Method and the Getting Thru Techniques (GTT) that she studied at the Awakenings Institute. She is also a Certified Dream Coach®, from the Dream University®. She now integrates her training as a musician and the use of high energetic vibrational frequency essential oils into her practice.

Sylvie offers different group and individual programs, online and offline. To learn more about her work and to tap into your highest frequencies, visit her website: www.goldenheartwisdom.com.

Chapter 2

Receiving Hidden Messages Guiding Your Life

By Cory Michelle

Everything has a message for you. *Everything.* Are you receiving the messages?

That's a pretty bold statement to claim, that everything, including people, objects, plants… everything is showing up to show you something. My question to you is: are you paying attention?

For my entire life I doubted my intuitive abilities and questioned my awareness. Everything I did was choosing against what my awareness was saying. I'd often say, "I knew that was going to happen!" Have you ever said that to yourself?

What was going on? Could I really be aware of the future? Could I really have already known what was going to be created?

What if I *could* perceive the future?

Why yes, I can. But I wasn't willing to know that.

What kinds of messages are you perceiving and ignoring?

Messages come in many forms: energetically, through our light & heavy, words from another's mouth, songs, knowings, repeat patterns showing up, random thoughts that pops into your head, and physical signs (literally or figuratively).

I began becoming aware of these messages after I was finally willing to acknowledge them. I was finally willing to know something beyond what was logical or made sense to linear thinking mind.

Now, after four years of playing with these messages and how I perceive them, I am living a totally different life. Everything is different, everything. But it took me willing to trust and acknowledge how aware I truly was for the change to occur.

So what does receiving these messages have to do with the energy of receiving?

If you are willing to be aware and trust you, you can see what every choice will create. You can see where you are choosing against yourself, or choosing to expand.

Let's look at some ways I use my awareness to receive more and to change my life.

Relationships

For years, I was dating the same man over and over; 10 men in different bodies but the same thing would show up. He would claim that he had 'committed' to me and then be seeing other women. I started to believe I was terrible at relationships, unlovable, and not someone worth being with. This was all heavy to believe. So I asked: *what is true here? What would it take to have someone in my life that is generative, a contribution, nurturing, kind and resonant with me?* When I asked these questions I became aware of an energy of what was possible. I said YES to that energy. I continued dating but this time found that within the first couple of emails or on the first date, the energy between the guy and I was NOT a match to the energy when I asked the previous question. Ah HA! In the past I would have ignored this and continued on because they were handsome or we had a nice time. This time I said no thank you, and asked the question again.

Within a couple months I met Brian, a match to the energy I was asking for.

Key: Notice where you perceive more heavy energy versus light energy. The lightness is where you choose and life expands. This is the hidden message!

We are taught to make choices based upon reason, logic, emotions, pros and cons. However, when you choose based on the lightness or match to the energy of what you are asking for, you can change anything in your life.

Money

What is your relationship with money like? Do you treat it like a decadent lover? Or like your worst enemy? What messages are you conveying to money? What messages is it giving back to you?

I realized at one point that money was not my priority. Instead, not having money was a priority. I believed that I didn't need money, I didn't care about it and quite frankly I didn't even know how to ask for it in my business. The truth: I was afraid of money. My side of my relationship with money was lacking considerably.

So, what was money saying to me?

Pay attention to me! Stop making me wrong or I'll go away. If you don't learn how to treat me you'll never have me.

How was this showing up in my life? Well, I usually had a $0 balance in my bank account, I accrued over draft fees, paid people late, always looked for a discount, spent money on junk, couldn't ask for business, and I ignored emails from people wanting sessions from me.

I was unwilling to receiving the messages. And more importantly, I was totally unwilling to perceive the energy of what *I could choose* that could create a different money reality.

I believed that I was bad with money. This belief had me

ignore any and all messages money had for me; all it wanted was for me to receive it.

So what did I do when I realized this was how I was operating? I chose to make money a priority and asked: *what can I know, be, perceive and receive about money that will open up my money flows and give me a greater relationship with money?*

The first thing I noticed was that I was refusing money. There were five people in my email inbox asking for sessions from me that I had not replied to in over a week. I replied and in came $1500.

Second, I noticed that I had not been paying attention to my bank account. So I started being conscious about where I was spending and receiving money. I chose to be grateful for every penny I spent and received. Before, I avoided checking my account due to the fear that nothing was there.

Third, I started asking money to be my friend, my lover and to play. I told it I was sorry for ignoring it for so long. The energy became lighter. My bank account began to grow as I continued to grow my relationship with money by releasing all fear and doubt that I could never have as much money as I desire.

Messages from money can be muddled with attachments and conclusions. If you believe that if you do X then Y will show up, then you'll trap yourself. The alternative is to choose the lightness. For example, I've had a few opportunities to make some money and even though everything seemed great, there was a heaviness around it. Whenever I ignored that and choose it anyway I'd either lose money or have invested in something that didn't create anything additional for my money flows. Now I always ask: *if I choose this, what will my life and money flows be like in 5 years?* Then I perceive the energy; is it light or heavy? Light will create more of that energy, heavy will create more heavy energy.

You can also ask other questions like:

If I choose this will it expand my business? If I choose this, will it expand my money flows?

Key: Be aware of when you are concluding that if something is light, it will for sure work out. Just because it's light doesn't mean it will work out the way you think or want. More often than not the Universe has another plan in store that may not look like what you think! Keep asking questions and following the energy. If the energy gets heavy at any point, you can ask another question and make a different choice.

Business

At one point in my entrepreneurial career, I had created a business that could have been a multi million-dollar business. However, due to me not being able to receive money, I instead created $150,000 of debt. When I began becoming aware of this concept of perceiving energy, and following the light & heavy, that business began to get heavier and heavier. Truth be told, it was likely already heavy but I wasn't willing to know it. I was very much attached to it making me rich. And I believed that it was going to be the thing I did for a very long time. But after 4 years of suffering, I began perceiving where the light energy was. The first time I realized it was when I was facilitating a few friends with the tools of Access Consciousness®. Everything in my world lightened up and realized that the message from this facilitation was that it was giving me more light energy! I asked: *what will it take to facilitate more?* The following day I received an invitation to facilitate a class in another state. Wow, that showed up fast! I said yes, even though I wasn't certified to teach this class. I created the opportunity for myself to get certified and facilitated the class. This lightness was just the beginning.

Questions to ask: *What would it take for me to know, perceive, be and receive what is generative for me?* Then choose when it shows up, even if it doesn't make cognitive sense.

Your Home and Things

Do you ever look at your kitchen or bedroom closet and think "Gosh I really should clean this up?" But instead of doing it right then, you ignore it and do something else? And THEN, do you make yourself wrong for being messy or lazy? Later you see the mess again and the same pattern occurs? What is your space telling you?!

I used to have this pattern with my kitchen. Every time I walked in "clean me" would scream from the dirty dishes in the sink, however I'd interpret as "Cory, you are so messy, you'll never be a neat and tidy person". Cute, huh? I just believed that I was messy, and that it was a part of my personality... or so I thought. One day I realized that it was the kitchen yelling at me to clean it. I chose to clean it and I could practically hear it say "Thank you!" The energy was so light in the house and in my body. Then, later that day I ended up getting 2 new clients! The messages from your home, space and stuff can come through in many ways. The way I typically begin with my clients is by asking: *what are you procrastinating or avoiding doing? When you look at that room what are you aware of? What thoughts arise? And what action could you take to change the energy?*

When you perceive what your space, home and stuff is communicating to you, everything can change in a moment. What was surprising to me was how I'd get new clients when I cleaned! When your space is in order (the way it would like to be) it will create with you and support you.

Questions to ask:

What is my space asking for that I can choose now?

What can I arrange to create more lightness in my reality?

What is asking to be moved?

Is there anything that no longer belongs here?

When you ask these questions, check in for the energy. What pops into your awareness first? Play with it, clean something, organize, arrange and perceive the change in energy. You'll start to notice when something is out of place, it will just feel off. When you move it, the item may seem to start to sparkle or glow.

Tip: This may sound crazy, but try talking to your stuff. See what it is all about and even ask: would you be willing to contribute to me? If it says no, you may consider selling it or getting rid of it.

Those are just a few examples you can do and ask to begin to play with, explore, and be curious about, the hidden messages in your reality. What are they? Where is the lightness?

What is being communicated to you that, if you were to perceive and choose, would change your life?

Consider that everything has consciousness and that everything is communicating with you all the time. That's a lot of information! Mostly we turn off our awareness by not trusting ourselves, doubting our awareness and trying to figure everything out. When you begin to perceive how much everything wants to contribute to you, you create ease. Are you willing to receive the hidden messages?

For more information about how to ask these questions, perceive the energy and hidden messages and change your life: http://corymichelle.us/.

ABOUT THE AUTHOR: *CORY MICHELLE*

Cory Michelle has an elegance with energy and space, her intuitive sense dives into the depth of an issue to unlock it in seemingly non related places that result in total life change. She is playful, fun, and of course juicy. She breaks the rules of your traditional business coach and helps you achieve the life you came to live, juice and all.

Cory Michelle has one target with every client she works with: to be the potency required for them to change anything. Who she be creates an invitation to shift any challenge, tune into the truth and pinpoint the root of any issue, to create the change one truly desires. Some say it's her magic but really, Cory Michelle's potency ignites your own magic in business, leadership, money and relationship quickly.

She is a facilitator with the dynamic body of work Access Consciousness and Radiant Design, seasoned entrepreneur, speaker, trainer and author. Cory plays with space and energy to assist people in creating the life they came to live.

Chapter 3

Seduced Receiving: Be the Gift You Truly Be

By Dr. Lisa Cooney

For the first two decades of my life I was extremely unhappy. In my early 20s, I tried to numb out. I drank, did drugs, and partied. I was overweight. I didn't care about myself. One night I almost died because of my reckless behavior.

You see, I grew up in a very violent household. I was abused sexually, physically, and emotionally, from the time I was a baby and even into my 20s.

This abuse took over my entire life. I felt guilty, helpless, and in terror all the time. Nothing I did seemed to help. Happiness was out of my reach. It seemed impossible to me to even live. The abuse had control over every aspect of my life.

Everything felt wrong, including me. I never felt like I fit in anywhere. The only thing that made me happy was alcohol and escaping: I would drink or snort anything I could get my hands on in order to not feel anything. This felt like the best way to exist: dazed and confused.

In college, I walked around campus with my eyes down and shoulders hunched. One day, the professor in my Family Violence class reached out to me and asked me if I was OK. Nobody had ever asked me this. Ever. My eyes immediately filled with tears.

This professor helped me realize that what I had been living with was treatable. She filled me with hope that I could get beyond this and create a new life for myself.

And that is what I've done. The abuse no longer has control over me. I've created a life for myself that is beyond anything I ever imagined.

I'm living my dream life: I travel for work and pleasure internationally. I am traveling and facilitating classes on being Radically Alive Beyond Abuse and Receiving Energy with our Bodies.

I live in a beautiful home in California that I share with my Enjoyable Other. I have intimate, nurturing and supportive relationships with friends and loved ones. I am healthy, vibrant, and strong.

I've committed the past 20 years of my life to helping others get free from the prison of abuse and create a meaningful and joyful life for themselves. I've worked with thousands of clients who rave about the brilliant results they get in working with me. They say my facilitation is balanced with potency, sexual-ness (the energy of receiving) and vulnerability.

At 45, I am happy. The happiest I have even been with me. I feel joyful, light, and free. I have finally received me and I keep on learning new ways to receive me.

Of course there were many steps I took after that fateful day in college when my professor reached out to me. It's not like receiving came to me overnight.

I want to share some of these steps with you, along with some simple yet powerful tips that you can put into practice today in support of experiencing deeper receiving in your own life.

I have shared these steps with thousands of my clients. Believe me, they work.

I overcame two decades of abuse and went on to create a life beyond my wildest dreams. If I can do this, you can do this too.

Whether or not you struggled with abuse, chances are, if you're reading this book, there is something in your life that feels like a trap, a cage, some way you feel locked out of the possibility of receiving.

The good news is the key to unlock the prison of not receiving you rests inside of you. I can help you find it and use it.

What is Receiving?

Receiving is an action you take with no barriers to anyone or anything. It is a space of vulnerability, of openness, and of oneness with everything. Receiving has no boundaries or obligations. It is not forced or demanded, it is simply a way of being the space of YOU in the energy of YOU as the consciousness of YOU!

To be the energy, space and consciousness of you imagine you are as big as the universe and the earth and in that bigness you are everything and nothing at the same time. As you are a part of it all there is a molecular communion that exists that includes awareness with and for and about everything.

The is energy I call receiving gives you total power, total choice, total awareness, total strength from the vulnerability of the willingness to be the biggest you there is. What would the world be like if we all lived as this space of energy?

And yet, the energy of receiving on this planet has been mired with wars, conflict, abuse and terror. That is NOT the energy of receiving.

Receiving creates; abuse destroys. Receiving generates; wars destroy. Receiving produces communion; conflicts form separations. Receiving builds sustainability; terror extinguishes choice.

To choose is to receive. To receive is to choose beyond the form and structure of this reality. Receiving then is the greatest weapon we all have to abolish outdated modes of being; simply by being the energy of total allowance!

What is the Energy of Receiving?

It is the energy that is required to live the life you desire. It is also the energy you may be blocking if you experienced any form of abuse.

How do you know if you're blocking the energy of receiving?

• You crave communion yet feel stuck in less-than-satisfying relationships.

• You desire success in your career yet have hit a plateau and don't understand why you aren't earning more.

• You dream of being vibrantly healthy yet struggle with some chronic condition.

Read on to discover the connection between receiving and abuse. Here are five steps you can take to unblock the energy of receiving in your life.

Step 1: Acknowledge the Invisible Porcupine

How often do you get prickly when someone comes towards you?

I call it being the "invisible porcupine." It's a phenomenon I know very well, both in myself and in the thousands of clients I've worked with over the past two decades.

You know where these quills come from? Your past abuse. Once upon a time the world wasn't safe for you so you created these quills as your best attempt to protect yourself. The quills worked well back then, they are just out-dated now.

Yet how much are you uninviting into your life with these quills?

Just like you hoped the quills would keep your abuser away, they now keep love, money, clients and all else at a "safe" distance. A safe distance blocks receiving as you are always looking out for when the catastrophe will occur.

Is it time to update your hard drive?

The first step to unblocking yourself from the energy of receiving is to acknowledge that you've been an invisible porcupine with quills armed and ready to defend 24/7. To acknowledge you actually have embodied a self-defense posturing for attack all the time.

Step 2: Weed Out Stories That Block Receiving

When you experienced abuse you were forced to "receive" something you didn't wish to receive. In that moment you created a story that it's not safe to receive. Any form of receiving: love, money, health, becomes dangerous. For me, receiving meant receiving judgment. Receiving meant doing what my mom said so she wouldn't beat me. Receiving meant being and living other people's realities with a desperate desire to get nurturance and love (which I never got, except in the form of money and objects and ultimately abuse).

What does receiving mean to you?

What stories have you told yourself about receiving that keep the quills in place?

Are you willing to let those stories go?

What/Who have you misidentified and misapplied as receiving that is actually defending?

Step 3: Recognize the Quills Hurt Both Ways

Just like the "quills" of the invisible porcupine point outwards and keep everything in life (love, money, health, etc.) at a "safe" distance, they also point inward and keep you from coming forward into your own life.

At some point, perhaps a long time ago, you learned it wasn't "safe" to come forward. In your attempt to escape your abuse, or tell someone about your abuse, you may have disconnected or dissociated. Either way, you went away from yourself to try to keep yourself safe.

So you keep poking yourself with your own quills in the form of judgments and stories that it's not safe to be seen or heard.

Do you know what the most painful thing about all of this? You're living your own life at a "safe" distance from yourself and never fully receiving the beauty and potency of YOU. You never get to RECEIVE you.

And frankly, you probably have little to no knowledge of who you be because you have always been the quills and never allowed the real you to emerge. That is the real epidemic of abuse in this reality. Us divorcing from us!

Just like Steps 1 and 2, you need to acknowledge the quills hurt you, too, and let go of the stories you have made about what it means to come forward in your own life.

Forgiveness and acceptance are the keys to this step. They are not for anyone but you, to forgive and accept yourself is the greatness kindness you can receive for you.

Step 4: Release Forced Receiving

As mentioned in Step 2, when you experienced abuse you were forced to "receive" something you didn't wish to receive. This is called "forced receiving."

How does this past experience impact how you give to others today?

Have you gotten away from forced receiving or are you actually repeating the cycle?

Forced receiving sets you up to be rejected again and again. It is what keeps you from true communion in every aspect of your life.

How do you know if you're trapped in the cycle of "forced receiving"?

You think you know what's best for others. ("Here, eat this." "Do this." "Take this.") You give what you think others "should" have instead of what they ask for.

Basically, you are living as superior to everyone and unaware about everything. Just because you can do things for others doesn't actually mean they wish for you to. Do you realize that by forcing someone to receive what you think it's best for them to have you are basically telling them you know better and are smarter and are more aware? That is a de-valuing of another and total disrespect of their being.

So stop forcing your will on others, and allow them to be who they be and receive them for all of it with no point of view. Simple curiosity about another goes a long way in creating relationships from receiving and allowing.

So how do you move beyond "forced receiving" and into another possibility?

Step 5: Embrace Seduced Receiving

It starts with awareness. Once you see how you are using "forced receiving" you can choose something else.

Yet what is beyond forced receiving?

Seduced receiving.

Seduction may seem dangerous to you, since you may have experienced abuse as a result of being or doing something that "seduced" another to force themselves upon you.

So just a reminder, like in Step 2, here you can choose to weed out this story that blocks you from receiving.

What if there's a "safe" way to be seductive?

And what if "seduced receiving" is essential to invite into your life all that you desire?

With seduced receiving you are being the invitation for what you desire. You become the energy of the possibility of greater health, relationship, money, and business.

What would it take for your kindness and gentleness to be so strong that it dissolved all the uncaring ways that you experienced (and that you continue to try to "protect" yourself against with your quills)?

It's in this place of seduced receiving that you truly be the gift you be: for yourself and the world. In this place of soft vulnerability you let go of the quills. There are no more barriers anymore.

In this place, the energy of receiving is flowing free and easy. In this place the space, energy and consciousness of receiving is vibrant, alive, potent, juicy and just plain yummy.

It's yummy because it's you being you. It's alive because you are embodying your energy. It's potent because your greatest strength is kindness. It's vibrant and juicy because you are allowing all of you to be gifted in and with this reality and that changes everyone and everything in and around you; molecularly.

Seduced receiving is the greatest form of vitality on this planet. And guess what? We all have it intrinsically.

So turn the switch on and let's activate the energy of receiving on this planet!

If not right now, when...

ABOUT THE AUTHOR: *DR. LISA COONEY*

Dr. Lisa Cooney is a leading authority on thriving after childhood sexual abuse. As a licensed Marriage and Family Therapist, certified Access Con-

sciousness Facilitator, Master Theta Healer and author of the upcoming books, *Kick Abuse in the Caboose: The Bridge to Radical Aliveness* and *When Did You Become a Slave to Abuse: Getting Free in a New Way.* She has supported thousands of people over the past 20 years move beyond their abuse to create infinite possibilities for themselves and joyful lives.

Lisa experienced sexual, physical and emotional abuse herself from the time she was a baby into her early 20s. Having found the key to unlock herself from the cage of abuse, Lisa has now committed her life to revolutionizing the approach to trauma. She is known for using pragmatic tools to create quantum change.

Dr. Lisa is an internationally sought-out facilitator and speaker and previously was the host of the radio show, "The Psychology of Soul," in which she interviewed well-known thought leaders such as Byron Katie. She was also interviewed on television on the topic of how individual healing impacts the collective.

Dr. Lisa's clients come to her seeking core healing. They end up feeling safe, gotten, and powerfully guided in a deep personal transformation. Her clients not only heal from their childhood sexual abuse, they move beyond abuse to create their living dream!

Visit her site to find out more about her Beyond Abuse Revolution and to access her Free Gifts: www.DrLisaCooney.com.

Chapter 4

Embracing the Ballerina/Dancer

By Angela Redman

Approaching the Ballerina
Sparkling in her delight
Feeling her movement / moving her to move…
Tears from within,
Taking her away
Onwards to that endless river of joy…
Observing and embracing the love,
The higher in her mind…
Accepting all,
In the face of truth
She is the Ballerina,
Sparkling in her delight
The stars are in her eyes,
Only the stars
Shining bright…
It's okay to feel the Ballerina
It's just a feeling of delight…

Waiting in my crib to be collected, I am alone anticipating my energy of receiving

"I want to understand this energy of receiving," whispered my two-week-old self. "It feels different to how I thought this would all feel."

I'm going to go with this, this will be love, I know love and I recognize love.

I am collected, I am now nurtured, and I am safe. I am bringing happiness and I like happiness. It's great to give this feeling away, the feeling of happiness. Basking in happiness, I am young, so very young.

Inside a precious jewelry box, there she was. When opened, she was so happy to delight. Timeless, beautiful, no questions asked. A pleasure that was hers and only hers alone. Captivated by just going to that jewelry box and seeing the Ballerina in all her delight.

It became her dream to be that Ballerina. So she said, "yes" to the Ballerina path, the path that felt light.

So here it is, I now have fully embraced this Ballerina path, my parts are incredibly beautiful to play. I am learning, really learning, all of these incredibly complex routines. So I breathe, breathe in real tight as I am the Ballerina, oh how it is to delight.

I now feel beautiful. I am one with my shared delight. This path is bright, so very bright. At times the light that is in my eyes blinds me. So the dancing takes flight, I am the dancer. I now know I will always be the Ballerina. I am young so very young, but oh how I can delight.

I see the Sun; I get to know this precious, precious Sun, I now merge into Sun almost every day of this life. To see the glorious Sun, oh how I now know you as my dearest friend. I am dazzled, dazzled how you are so big, giving, so incredibly warm, incredulous with the life force. Friend, you are my dear friend. I will always love you Sun, the recipient of your receiving.

I will always be yours dear Sun; I am so filled with emulating your gifts. Unconditional is so very limiting. So I dance through the Ballerina as I accept her part to play. So it is with honouring this gentle, shy Ballerina I will emulate you. I will give this Sun-ship from my heart; I will give it over and over again as I an endless, infinite. I am this endless receiver, the gift of receiving no words can describe at times…

Our paths have many different opportunities to step into our heart truth at any given moment, how is your Ballerina showing up?

Then the emotions of guilt arrived, a guilt that was true, but it had love attached, how was this so true? It's only small, but I will receive this, it's my gift… That I know is true.

When I was able to walk on and walk into more of the happiness, it was colourful, very colourful. Love is very intoxicating. I wanted to receive this most glorious happiness, a non-tangible phenomenon. A phenomenon that I believed was true...

"Breathe, breathe in this beauty."I claimed it is my gift. This feels glorious, so very right, so I can receive this feeling, however it is not mine alone anymore. It's full, it's full of judgments, emotions, feelings. I'm now travelling on a new road, it has love, only small, but it has love. I am receiving this, it is my gift and I have gratitude for this. I claim my receiving.

Surrendering is so much easier than numbing the voice down as it requires much courage, bravery and self-belief of that!

I love how the dancer within always wants to dance with us all of the time, sometimes slowly, sometimes fast and even very still. Stillness, I love the stillness dancer, so strong, nourishing, a comfort within is the stillness dancer. She can contemplate, gather, redirect, understand and integrate all the small steps to the dance. To dance in perfectly perfect receiving. Receiving, oh how I love the Energy of Receiving!

I now have the sky, so much potential to reach, it's right there in front of me, oh how much I'm in delight. My limitless potential it's floating above me, I just need to keep looking up. How beautiful is this potential, oh how I weep with effervescent joy.

Dancing is natural we simply feel our rhythm. What message is my world singing to me? What dance do I feel to respond with?

My piece is only my piece, in the Greater Dance. I make a difference. Sometimes I am quiet, sometimes I am incredibly bright, and I am in my dance. I am dancing for the life.

It is now time to embrace, embrace my world, a world enriched with such beauty and unseen places, it is time to delight.

Here comes the time now, this is my true receiving, it is her, she is my child, oh how she is my delight. I am grateful, she is only small, but its love, I recognise love…

We now share the journey of receiving, I receive the receiving. I am blessed, blessed so very high. I am grateful, she now doesn't cry.

Here comes the new receiving, oh wow this is not small love, and it's big, so much bigger. I now accept this and relish upon the receiving.

I am now scared, I have this love, the energy of receiving and I am now breaking down.

Wait, here he comes, it's a boy, my child. I can receive again, this is my gift. I accept, I am so very grateful.

I'm practicing now very big receiving. It is true, very true, I know this, I recognise love...

I look for love, its everywhere around me. It is so very beautiful opening the door of love. Love has many colours, I'm addicted to this love, love is now addicted to me.

I was not born of love, I did not realize that I was love, the timeless love that permeates and surrounds us. Can you be love, feel the love? Hold the love...

My star is always bright, so very bright. I had at times taken her down, down to rest. "Rest" I said, "my star". Receive the energy of receiving, that I can do.

So I surrender to you "receiving"... I love you! I am receiving you, I am the happy receiver.

We are the endless receiver's of receiving. We choose our receiving.

So what can I choose here right now, to the endless choosing of receiving. Which do I choose?

My journey home to the simple Ballerina is an everyday choice. It's a very simple choice. Do I dance to this movement with this moment or do I just dance away? Beyond?

I am the dancer, the perfect dancer of my life. It is my own dance. I am slow, I am fast, I can bend and at times break, I am the gifted receiver. I accept the receiving.

The love I now receive has become very big love now. I accept this love, I recognise love. I am receiving this greater love. It is okay, to know. It is not too much to receive. It is absolutely fine to know it's your gift to be gifted with the energy of receiving, big, very big, small, micro, it's an abundant universe constantly sending out lots of gifts for you in every moment.

The universe has an endless giving nature. Oh how I love, thank you universe for being patient on learning your very giving nature so incredibly abundant that you are.

So what's my capacity in this moment to the energy of receiving? How will you interpret your dancer? Only we can really decide and accept our true capacity for receiving. Giving is our very innate natural nature. Receiving is an art to learn, explore, grow into and understand.

The gifts of allowing others to gift you their energy makes for a very happy receiver. I declare to you I have become the happy receiver, the receiving of my own full and embodied star. A practicing star of self-love. I am choosing to be my star performer, in my own expression of my dance, coming together with all, in sharing, being a creative happy receiver. May I dance with you?

I choose happiness, I choose peace, I am peace, and I seek peace. Peace is seeking me.

I Embrace Wellness… my wellness.

Love, from the practicing receiver.

ABOUT THE AUTHOR: *ANGELA REDMAN*

Angela Redman was born and adopted in the City of Adelaide, South Australia where she has grown up and spent her life, thus far. The capital of South Australia, Adelaide has historically been the hub of free-spirited and free-thinking people. Adelaide was the first place to abolish sexual and racial discrimination, the first to do away with capital punishment, the first to recognise Australian Aboriginal land rights, the first to give women voting rights.

Adelaide has also been nicknamed the City of Churches. Although it is not known as to who first started using this nickname, one only needs to take a look around to dig out the rationale behind such a nickname. Churches boasting exquisite architectural designs abound in this beautiful city with the Holy Trinity Anglican Church being the oldest which was built in the year 1838. With the increment in population, the number of churches enjoyed a huge boost over time.

Adelaide is reportedly the home to the biggest display of Aboriginal Culture and artifacts. These are showcased at the South Australian Museum as well as at Tandanya – the National Aboriginal Cultural Institute.

Angela is a mother of two, Wellness Coach, Healer, Intuitive, Model, Dancer for Life, Yogini, Author, Nature Lover, Passionate Cook, Community Hugger, and Happiness Promoter.

Angela loves to cook, eat, and enjoy the art of self-care in her own time with her family. She has always been a passionate student observer of life and is an active member of expanding and sharing the rising and raising of our consciousness in her beautiful city and community.

Angela's training includes Reiki, Intuitive Guidance, Everyday Practical Aromatherapy, Australian Bush Flower Essence Therapist, Certified Cookery, Family and Wellbeing Counselling, Crystal Therapy, Meditation, Indian Head Massage, Pranic Healing, Polarity Therapy, Global Happiness Networker, Gym Instructor, Life Style Consultant, Wellness Coaching, and Holistic Counseling for Body Mind and Spirit.

Angela is fortunate to be available in locations in Adelaide where she can offer her skills to all people in her city. Angela has been operating her business "Embracing Wellness" since 2007. You can receive Embracing Wellness through an in-person session, Skype session, social media or via these web sites: www.embracingwellness.com.au or www.facebook.com/embracingwellness. Contact Angela directly via email on angeladman@embracingwellness.com.au.

Are you ready to receive Embracing Your Wellness?

Chapter 5

Insanity: The Adventure of Letting Control Go

By Rebecca Hulse

There's something about the energy of receiving that is truly balls to the wall, scary. Terrifying. A total lack of control it seems. Who knows what could show up? What if the universe hates me? What if I receive ugly presents all the time? What if I actually got what I really desire? What then? What would I do?

What's really insane is that none of that is true. Take a look at it - Is it light and expansive when you read it? Or is it heavy and contracted? There's a heavy intensity to it - it's judgment, conclusion… something you've already decided that receiving is.

Is that it really though? Or is it something entirely different that perhaps you have never been willing to see?

Gary Douglas, the founder of Access Consciousness® has told me time and time again "When you choose judgment you can have no other possibility." Judgment is literally the cutting off of receiving and nothing can change. If nothing can change, can you ever have the possibilities of the future that would surprise and delight you beyond what you could ever imagine?

In the *Big Bad(ass) Book of Judgment* I received dramatic and accurate information about how judgment really creates your reality:

> *"Every judgment is the energetic equivalent of a pianist slamming down the lid on his hands after a bum note. A speaker zipping her lip after hearing words she doesn't like. A writer snapping her pencil because of a spelling mistake (a pencil...really?). A dancer walking out of class after forgetting the choreography. A runner chucking out her shoes because she didn't beat her last time or a mother giving away her kids because she was tired and yelled at them."*

This drama has a lot of intensity, but it shows a lot of the insanity that choosing judgment over receiving truly is. It's the off button. There's a level of insanity with judgment that totally eliminates the possibility of receiving and how you could choose a different possibility. And judging the judgment perpetrates the cycle.

How insane is that? Anyone else feel like they're running in a hamster wheel?

When you have been functioning from the polarity of judgment, consciously or more likely not, it's hard to even look at what the other possibilities could be without context. Sense and be aware of the energy of judgment. Now, is that really what you are interested in having, being and creating for your life? Or is there a different possibility?

Now from this space of awareness, could you tap into the energy of receiving? Does it open up a space in your body, being and reality? I wonder what your life could be like in five years if you chose more of that?

Judgment and receiving have a true relationship - from a dictionary sense. Relationship defined in an Oxford English pre-1936 dictionary is described as:

"The distance between two objects."

How much do you have to cut off and separate you from everything else, to function from judgment? How much energy does that take, I wonder? As an infinite being could you truly ever be separate from anything?

And for what reason would you want to be?

One of the gifts of receiving is that you always have a sense of communion with everything - the sense of separation most human beings have here on earth, (like loneliness, angst, and honestly, misery) comes from using your energy to separate yourself.

There's this crazy belief that if you're separate you finally get to be you and then be happy, but the more you separate the more you cut off everyone, including you and the communion. In other words, your receiving is eliminated.

Insanity? Yes, now we're getting somewhere...

This beautiful planet and every being and energy on it is constantly contributing to you. But if you are walking around in your little dog cone of separation (like when your pet gets fleas), the contribution around you bounces off. You're left to walk around like nobody cares, because nothing can get through your barriers unless you choose to allow it to, potent being.

Maybe you're interested in using the amazing potency you be to your advantage? Which would include receiving you and all the contribution the world is waiting to gift to you?

The exciting possibility is that you can actually have a different reality right now. What if you sensed the way the earth functions and receives - naturally, easily and with no judgment. What would it take for you to have more of that?

What about playing with this? Bring the energy of the earth receiving into your body - literally introduce it to all the spaces between the molecules of your body (not very big) and now of your being (bigger than you could imagine).
"Hi body, hi receiving, hi being, hi earth."
This process starts to introduce you to one of the ways you naturally function - acoustically. It's funny to me the amount

of requests I get to help people with their 'Receiving Problem'. The problem is never receiving but that you're not willing to be.

It also doesn't help that this lifetime might be the first time in trillions of years that you're actually willing to receive. So instead of now throwing everything away and destroying yourself in the process - how can you ease yourself into something that you haven't functioned from in forever?

One of my favorite quotes so far from The Golden Planet (also by Gary Douglas) is *"There is no destruction necessary for creation, only the need to request change."*

Would you be willing to create and out-create your capacities with Being, Knowing, Perceiving and Receiving? Is now the time?

Tapping into the acoustical wave of the earth - what you hear in live music, the energy and space you sense in nature, the crash of the wave at the beach is a natural example of receiving. This is one way you can start to play with the energy. Human Beings are not so great at receiving as a natural way of functioning at this point in time. But it is a capacity you do have - that you may have never ever chosen before... How exciting!

My question to you is: Would you be willing to have this crazy adventure and give up your control? I'm a control freak of magnitude, I do admit (I've been called out on it publicly), so I did my own testing.

I tried my way, where I controlled everything into what I thought I desired and created what I thought I wanted to happen… and it did work to a certain extent. But it requires a lot of time, energy and effort, things not relevant when you're functioning as an infinite being.

Then I gave up and said "OK Universe, what do you have for me? You obviously like the contribution I be because you haven't dropped a crane on my head, so what else is possible I have never considered before?"

And bam. Magic started to show up (and still does).

The cool thing about choosing receiving over control is that receiving never shows up the way you think it's going to! And it's never the same as anyone else. Even if you tried to duplicate the capacity someone else has with receiving, it would still be different. Could we ever all function the same? Or would our being permeate everything? This is why some bodies work really well with yours and others don't.

I see this a lot in the Access Consciousness® community where people compare their levels of 'receiving' which is total utter bulls***. Strong Talk inserted here! You've been warned!

Seriously - how can receiving ever be compared? Yes, there are a lot of people choosing not to receive and they may never. But is your judgment (often thinly masked as "Your Awareness") truly ever going to open a door to receive in the future?

Comparing receiving is like trying to find identical freckles - pointless and not generative. Instead, what if when you saw someone doing something interesting or creating something you haven't yet - you tapped into or duplicated in your own way their capacity with receiving?

Note: Please don't duplicate their entire reality. You may not like that. Duplicating their capacity with XYZ might create more of what you're looking for.

When you duplicate others' capacities with what you'd like to create you get to create more of a Meg Ryan reality of *"I'll have what she's having."* Instead of *"Let me cut off everything that's brilliant and working for me because it's obviously not creating that, which is what I want, which they have, so therefore I must need to be them..."*

More insanity right?

So what would it take to choose to increase your own awareness of receiving through duplicating others capacities? I wonder....

(You could also sense into the energy of what that could be like for you right now and bring that into every space between your molecules....)

If you're now stepping into questioning and really head tripping around "Well, how do I receive then?" Remember this catching, biblical phrase: "Ask and you shall receive." Did you know that amazing universal law that actually works? The real question is: What are you asking for?

More conclusion? Judgment? Limitation? Illusions? Lies and Confusion?

Or possibility? Your true capacities? The willingness to have all of you? To be so unstable that even your own limitations can't hold out for very long?

Every day you're having thoughts, feelings and emotions that aren't actually yours - 99 percent of them. You're the most brilliant radio receiver for beings on the planet but do you have this point of view that you have all these problems and you can't receive?

Or... did you just receive 99 percent of everyone else's reality and bought it as so real and true and yours that you have no space to even wonder what receiving you would really be like?

You might have heard of this wonderful tool called "WHO.

DOES.THIS.BELONG.TO?" and I'm probably not the first one to introduce you to it either... My question is: have you chosen it? And will you ever choose it?

Perceive a thought or feeling you have right now: Truth, is that yours, someone else's or something else's?

Now another one - yours, someone else's or something else's?

And another, yours, someone else's or something else's'?

Will you return all those to sender, with consciousness attached? Now what is happening in your world? Did that create a space in your being to receive the energy, space and consciousness you truly be? Receiving is something you're doing already! Maybe you're just not willing to receive you?

Did you ever find it's easier to help someone else rather than yourself? Like cleaning up someone else's home or perceiving their needs? But what about you? If you're not recognizing that 99 percent of what goes into your head isn't actually yours, there's no space to receive you, what you could create; what you require and desire.

We're taught in an emergency to put our own emergency mask on before others, otherwise you die suffocating and are no good to anyone! Have you ever wondered about applying that to the rest of your life? What if instead of catering your life to the needs, tugs and pulls on you from everyone else – you chose to be you and make you your first priority? And contributed to others from the space that you be? Would you might actually get to be happy? Something I noticed when I stop catering to anyone else's limitations and begin choosing happiness, is that from that space, just having a conversation with me can change someone else's reality. Just my smile becomes enough, or seeing a post on Facebook from me suddenly changed their entire day.

Now isn't that easier than running around after everyone? What if you being, knowing, perceiving and receiving was enough? For everyone – you included? (This also probably has nothing to do with the fact that you're humanoid… right? Well… let's not go there today).

So now what? If this lit you up and made your reality lighter, this may be true for you. Here is where you can make a demand and choose it. "No matter what it looks like, no matter what it takes I'm having this for me."

I wonder how it will show up for you? Are you willing to have it surprise and delight you… and be totally out of control… Really? Really? Really?

I wonder what else is possible when you get off your master control chair, switch off the auto-pilot that you programmed so well, and let the lightness guide you.

Where would you end up? What adventure into the energy of receiving would you create? What grand and glorious adventure would you have? Don't let it be easy...

Or fun.

Definitely don't do that...

ABOUT THE AUTHOR: *Rebecca Hulse*

Be careful ...she's a red-headed reality shake with a big bad crush on Iron Man! She's also a Playmate of Possibilities, BS buster, showers adoration on science fiction, and has a target to invite 10,000 or more brilliant beings to choose their brilliance and capabilities. Her knack for tackling the taboo subject of sex by separating myth from possibility is palpable.

From a 12-year old firewalker to 20-something reality shaker, human dynamics writer, entrepreneurial siren, and Access Consciousness Facilitator, Rebecca Hulse is an epicenter of her own earthquake style coaching. In between her fire walk moment, the Kiwi globe-trotting risk taker became a professional ballerina, published three books, taught Laughter Yoga, danced on the high seas with Royal Caribbean, loved and let go of the love of her life, launched her own international coaching practice in 2004, led workshops for Find My Genius in her hometown of Christchurch, New Zealand, and got certified as a trainer for Access Consciousness. These are only a few of the milestones achieved by this 21st century millennial wise woman created.

Rebecca Hulse is an ongoing work in progress and walking proof that "impossible is temporary" in a body. At 13 she began a career as a public speaker and to date has spoken to 300 teens on the power of choice to make their dreams a reality. By age 20, every item on her "bucket list" was checked off so she began creating a new one with a godzillion more adventures to accomplish. So far the results have been fast and fantastic. Read on.

From her cozy Christchurch home in New Zealand, Rebecca Hulse reaches and often traipses to a global audience from Australia, Canada, the Caribbean, the US, and Europe. How did it happen? She never believed in limitations. Instead, the possibilities have always been endless in her point-of-view. Her first two decades on planet Earth yielded a multi-faceted communications career spanning every genre: words, movement, workshops, dance, and beyond. Rebecca has loved, seduced, and ravished life and it's returned the same to her multiple times.

Her writing has been featured in *MindBodyGreen, NotSalmon, Wild Sister, My Yoga Online, Elephant Journal, Girlfriendology, Classy Career Girl, TeraWarner.com,* and *AccessConsiousness.com* just to name a few. So far, she has published three books:

Love Me For Real – Self-care You Will Actually Do (and Want To): If you are ruthlessly authentic in the art of self-cherishing, everything and everyone else will mirror it back to you. http://tinyurl.com/LMFRbook

The Big Bad(ass) Book of Judgment: Three days in a book from Rebecca's workshop to break free of judgment and feel free with life. Plunge into a deep dive on the roots of why you judge, how it limits you more than anyone or anything else, and discover how opportunities are endless when judgment is gone. www.rebeccahulse.com

69 Shades of Pleasure: The Manual You Should Have Been Given at

18: Throw out everything you think you know or learned about in 50 Shades of Gray. Read this instead. Just do it. Co-authored with Liam Phillips, creator of Curing the Incurable. https://www.amazon.com.au/dp/B00IVPMSEM

In 2014 she was certified as an Access Consciousness facilitator in Costa Rica, and promptly took her reality shaking mantra on the road in North America as a guest coach. She co-facilitated *"5 Days of Change – Life Will Never Be the Same"* with fellow Access Consciousness® facilitator Katherine McIntosh in Denver. Then she teamed up with Canadian facilitator Julia Sotas to become a dynamic duo and produced and launch the original virtual teleseries *"Living Beyond Disney"*. During their four live explorations, Rebecca and Julia explored the concept of finding Prince Charming as just one option for making the quantum leap towards the life you want. They busted fairy tales into oblivion and the result was: more ease for participants in the moment plus increased awareness of the bountiful opportunities to create a dream life with or without someone walking in to do it for you.

With a soul craving for change, Rebecca continues to challenge her expertise and talents to even greater possibilities. She says exactly what she thinks. Whether it's to bust a client's stubborn and limiting perceptions of reality or stirring the minds of many, Rebecca applies the Access Consciousness tools like pyromaniacs play with fire: let's just say your old points-of-views are burned to dust so a new paradigm can be created from choice instead of an old story about your "past".

Thanks to her dance background, Rebecca is a master of embodiment who also utilizes her training as an Access Bars and Body Facilitator to integrate and shift her client's mind-body connection simultaneously. Many testimonials echo the mantra: "In 10 minutes, Rebecca has turned around jobs, shifted paradigms and released judgments – forever."
Rebecca's ongoing romance with life continues even when she's not

coaching you out of the prison of your own mind. She is a ravisher of champagne, dances to her delight for joy and exercise, appreciates art, travels to new worlds, follows fashion like a Vogue Editor, and watches *"Once Upon A Time"* as she conjures up her dreams into realities all day and night.

How do you join the Playmate of Possibilities in playing with her on crazy adventures? Are you ready to shake off your reality and choose another more enchanting one? Is it time now to make your heart sing with the life you live? You can find Rebecca on Facebook at www.facebook.com/Rebecca.hulse.coach or on her website www.rebeccahulse.com.

Chapter 6

You Are Already Receiving: How Your Thoughts Actually Work

By Ken Elliott

For many years now, I have felt compelled at times to ask friends or strangers to make a wish. Well before I ever wrote the book *Manifesting 123,* I knew what thought could do and had a direct understanding of how it actually works. I was like the little Johnny Appleseed of asking. Without going into detail, I would simply suggest to people that they make some wishes. Lots of wishes.

People would get a little flustered or excited. I would quickly put them at ease and ask what they would desire in their lives. I would guess that only 20 percent of the people questioned were already asking for themselves.

The other 80 percent were approximately split in this way: Half would offer that they ask for things all the time but not for themselves. They're big hearted and generous, always thinking of their friends and families first. "I'm fine," they say and make improving the lives of everyone else a priority. It's a little uphill to get them to think of themselves first, but with some smiles and a little friendly nudging, many will give it a try.

The other half don't ask, but surprisingly, they're open to talk about it. The conversation usually flows easier than with the others. I've never met anyone that says, "I don't ask and I don't want to discuss it." People in this group are hopeful at their core and open to paths of positive outcomes but they put obstacles in the way.

"I used to ask for things but they came true and it scared me."

"I don't know what to ask for."

"I really don't have the time to think about it."

"Who am I supposed to ask?"

"I can give it a try but I don't think it matters."

"My imagination is not that good."

Sometimes during these conversations there is the silent

pause and I gently offer, "I know why you don't ask." Then I get the look and I kindly say back, "Because you're not worthy."

A quick reaction follows: laughter, a tiny flash of self-anger and sometimes an epiphany. They have been touched to their very core and some grab a chair to support themselves. Others burst into tears hearing their unworthiness spoken aloud. The thought of unworthiness is one of the greatest barriers to asking or manifesting. Because of people's belief that they are "less than," they will not ask for themselves. They are not good enough to receive.

But you are most worthy.

Over the years I have been blessed with a number of very gifted friends in my life. One of them, Judy Goodman, taught me about manifesting in a most unusual way. As an intuitive, Judy has a number of remarkable gifts including the ability to see thoughts and how they create our reality. When I first heard about this, I asked her if we could experiment with the concept.

She agreed, and for many years I would think of different things to send her just by thinking of them. I would picture an object in my mind for a few seconds and mentally send it off to her. Afterwards I would give her a call and ask her to describe what I had sent. Unbelievably, she accurately described what I sent her every time! We were 2,100 miles apart at the time, but distance had no effect on the experiment.

What an amazing game we played for all those years. I didn't know how this worked, but I suspected it was Judy's psychic ability. I never considered it could be something I was doing.

Later I became close friends with William Bulhman, the esteemed author and teacher of out-of-body experiences. Some call this astral travel, a way of leaving your physical body behind and traveling out beyond the physical world we live in.

In a conversation with William, we talked about the use of wish lists and vision boards. He always had a wish list going and his lists were dramatically successful. He talked about going to the 'other side' and seeing the items on his wish list arrayed in different stages of creation. He was describing how his thoughts were literally building things first in the non-physical realm. I was stunned.

William is an adept out-of-body traveler, going to what we call the other side a number of times each week. While traveling out-of-body, he would sometimes see the items on his wish list lined up and in various stages of development. The newest items on his wish list appeared to be wisps of vapor, poorly formed and very transparent. As these items developed, they would begin to take on a more three-dimensional form. All that was required to "grow" these items was more thought, more layers of intention and gratitude. It sounds a bit like growing a plant: You visit and water it.

William learned that by adding more thought and intention, the item would progress from a wisp to a more solid looking form with a blush of color. Apply more intention and the object would then become fully formed, completely 3-D and in full color. The fully formed object showed him that his wish list item would soon come into the physical world. The object would become more solid in proportion to the attention he gave it. It was easy to track the progress of the wish list item by seeing how solid it was. In his out-of-body travels, William was visiting his personal wish factory!

I had been sending numerous things to Judy Goodman for over a decade, but I had no idea I was creating these objects on my own. I never dreamed there was such a simple mechanism involved. I talked with Judy about what I recently learned from William and she confirmed that our thoughts literally build around us, unseen by us before they become physical. As I said in my book, this is one of the keys to the kingdom. It is incredibly important for you to embrace and put this to use.

With this information I fully understood what so many had said, "Mind is the builder, thoughts are real, your mind creates." I learned something those writers didn't know: how our thoughts literally build and create anything.
Thoughts are a natural law like gravity. Here's an example.

Hold an object out over the floor and let it go – it will fall to the ground every time because of the pull of gravity. Gravity will consistently pull everything to the ground. It is the law of gravity. Your understanding of gravity or your belief systems have no effect on water running downhill. Gravity doesn't judge you as a good or bad person or judge what you'll be using gravity for. Gravity is your birthright and gravity simply pulls things to the ground on a very consistent basis. It is the law.

Thought is a law as well. Your thoughts consistently make things all the time. It makes perfect sense that the objects around us are built a bit at a time and not suddenly conjured from a magician's hat. Your thoughts actually build in response to your efforts. Everyone is an expert at using their thoughts to manifest things. Further, we have been manifesting all our lives but most of us have been unaware of it.

It doesn't matter if you believe this information or not, or if you are a good or bad person. Your success in manifesting is not predicated on your abilities, IQ, or worthiness. Regardless of what you believe or understand, your thoughts continue to build things in response to your mind's instructions. Thought is a law and thoughts just build things.

Now you know how your thoughts begin to form objects and even concepts in the unseen world around you. Knowing this, you are free to change your life or not. You do not have to ask permission from anyone because creating from thought is your birthright. It is one of your greatest gifts in this life.

When you wake in the morning, do you fervently ask permission to breathe? Do you scramble around to find the air pockets you need to survive? Of course not. Breathing is your birthright and without it we could not live. Breathable air is around us all the time and we can use it to do what we wish.

Before you were even born it was pre-arranged for you to breathe the air and stand on this planet without flying off into space. It was also allowed that your mind could conceive and create things that you require and hope for.

We are not perfect and, fortunately, that is not the point of our being here. We make mistakes; we fail and crash to the ground at times. This is how we learn.

Whatever your history to this point, it has not taken away your worthiness. The harshest people can become the greatest examples. Their potential for good, their worthiness was always in place.

I would wish for you perfect health, happiness and living comfortably. You wouldn't have to work just to survive, you would have a life without struggle. Then, if you have all that you require, you would have the luxury of time and resources to help others.

I would wish that you ask for yourself first and simply receive.

Since creating with thought is your birthright, don't hesitate to bring good things to yourself and share the abundance.

Remember that manifesting is not dependent upon your belief system or your worthiness. You do not have to possess any special skills or gifts. All that is required is that you ask and continue to revisit the same intention every day. Just once a day is enough.

A lot of thinking has been put into the act of receiving. Yes, it can be said that we can get in the way of the process, but keep in mind that thoughts just build things regardless. If you are manifesting that perfect career and have a nagging concern that you are not capable, what is happening? You are building two separate outcomes. Your thoughts will begin working on both scenarios and revisiting them each day will build both of them. You can successfully get that perfect job and subsequently be fired or demoted. Congratulations on making two things at once! Your thoughts won't cancel each other out because they were two separate ideas on two separate tracks.

Were you ready to receive the new career? And how about the demotion? Your thoughts simply build things, and ready or not, they are building anyway.

When you post a letter, it is on his way. If you mail a letter self-addressed to yourself, it is routing back to you. It is not going to wait for your readiness, it arrives on its own schedule.

When you were using your thoughts to manifest, your idea is being created as efficiently as possible. If you are imagining that perfect partner, then there may be quite a few moving parts to arrange. To make a space for you there may be changes in that other person's life, you may need to meet someone to make the introduction or you may need a bit more time for some personal improvement. In this case, your thoughts are creating the perfect outcome efficiently but time is required for people to be moved around or for a bit more "polishing up."

If you are asking and manifesting, then it is building. Avoid any concern about your readiness or worthiness. Like the air you breathe, all is ready for your every thought to begin building your wishes. Now let's improve the efficiency of making those dreams come true.

Quite simply, the process is this: Imagine you are in your future and all that you specify has already happened. Your thoughts can actually build the future, so take full advantage. There is no need to figure out everything that has to fall into place. You simply imagine that you are there and all is just the way you want it. Walk around in it and use your senses to breathe and smell the air. Put yourself in the scene and increase the sensation of being in the lovely future you desire. Remember, keep it simple and don't specify how this wonderful future came to be. It doesn't matter how it happened. Like a scene in a move, just imagine being in your perfect future every day. Your thoughts will immediately start to work on the idea, becoming more and more solid in the field around you. Eventually what you build will come into your physical world. Then, empower your good intention, this future, with one of the two great forces, love or fear. In your lovely future, take the time to express your gratefulness. While you're at it, thank God or the God of your understanding for making this all possible. It leaves you with a nice feeling and besides, it's just good manners. Adding gratefulness is the multiplier; it is the quickest way to success.

Equally important, and it must be offered here, is how to handle worries, which are thoughts that create as powerfully as your happy ones.

Your worries are thoughts charged with fear. If you worry, you are creating outcomes in the same way. We can't afford to create negative scenarios or go backwards in our lives.

Here's the fix.

To combat fearful thoughts, you will typically hear some version of "Don't worry about it so much," in an attempt to diminish the negative idea. Other suggestions sound like,

"It could be worse," and "It will be OK."

Instead, be pro-active and convert your worries to action items. If you are worried about those bills to pay, off-load that worry to your calendar as a to-do item. On your calendar or smart phone, note that at 9 a.m. Monday, you will be reminded to make a call and ask your boss for a raise. At 6 p.m. that night, you will note to call people who owe you money. On Tuesday evening, you will make a time to contact a mentor about a better career path or that old business idea. What you are doing is moving the emotion of fear onto a calendar listing for another day. You will take action on that money concern at an appropriate time, not in the middle of the night when you are in worry and fear. Taking action is a positive. You are expanding the possibilities for success and meeting these problems constructively. Pat yourself on the back!

You are the recipient of all you think. You are the responsible party and you have created your present life. Your life continues to unfold around you day by day, thought by thought. You have been doing this all your life so you are already expert at manifesting, it is your life's work. You are constantly receiving what you think.

Now you have the knowledge and tools to create great things for yourself. Design and build your heart's desire and make your life even better.

Be good to yourself. Point yourself to happiness.

Ken Elliott
www.manifesting123.com

Judy Goodman
www.judygoodman.com

William Buhlman
www.astralinfo.org

ABOUT THE AUTHOR: *KEN ELLIOTT*

Ken Elliott is an author and artist living in Castle Rock, Colorado. He has experienced and collected astonishing stories for more than 25 years. In a unique and convincing way, Ken learned how thought works, continually building objects and concepts in the unseen field around each of us.

Ken is an accomplished speaker, passing this empowering information on to individuals and groups. For more information on Ken's lectures and workshops, email ken@manifesting123.com or visit www.manifesting123.com.

Chapter 7

Keep the Light On, I'm Coming Home
The Gift of an Open Heart

By Robyn M James

I am consciously overwhelmed
By the love that is,
By the healing that is taking place,
By my will to surrender.

And I weep from this place of love
For all who do not yet recognise love,
Who do not know it is theirs, and
Who are not yet willing to surrender…

Come bathe with me in the love
Come see yourself as the light.
And in the presence of such love
And with the guidance of your own light,

Choose to see me
Choose to meet me
Choose to understand me,

For though we are each other,
our uniqueness asks for recognition.

If you cannot see me
And you do not wish to see me,
I surrender, and
I ask love that you will (to) see yourself,

That is most important.

—from I AM SURRENDER © 2012

Stuart: You keep talking about coming home. I haven't even left yet.

Joy: I see that. I see you have never left. You know, I think that if you go looking for yourself, you will find yourself. I'd just about guarantee it.

Stuart: What do you mean, *just about*?

Joy: Well, I cannot account for your resourcefulness, your determination, your clarity of intention, or your effort.

Stuart: Oh! So you're suggesting I have to do it a certain way?

Joy: No, my child…

She paused. Many times in the excitement of her passionate enthusiasm, Joy had done way more than simply acknowledge that life was an invitation to take whatever adventure was most appealing to the traveller. She was a pioneer of her own path and the amazing gifts and treasures she had consciously uncovered were presents she wanted everyone to receive. She was so liberated by the lessons and insights she had gained along the way that she had a tendency to want to inspire others by insisting they understand her lessons, as if she had discovered some universal truth.

She was learning to stay true to her own path; it had occurred to Joy that everyone was a pioneer, a potential seeker of their own truth. And just as the universe had completely supported her every step of the way, Stuart's providence lay in wait.

But she could not say nothing – what would be the point of that?

Joy searched her heart for loving words that would balance her passion with a greater wisdom.

Joy: Stuart…there are no rules, only choices. Not unexpectedly, your journey will be filled with treasures, some shiny and inviting, some hidden in the darkness. Do not be deceived to value one more than the other; do not mistake your path as easy or hard; and do not be so sure as to where your enemies hide. Do, by all means, come to know yourself as a spiritual warrior.

Stuart: I'm not leaving you, you know?

Joy: I know. You'll never leave me... that is pretty well guaranteed.

It seemed another question about guarantees was about to arise, so she quickly offered unemotional parting words.

Joy: It appears you have everything you need, so I wish you well. Enjoy your journey, child.

Stuart: Keep the... *light on...*

She had already left the room.

The story of joy is the story of love. And it is nothing less than a remarkable inward quest of transformation.

It was love that beckoned me forth to consciously choose this journey. I must admit, I didn't know that at the beginning. At age 24, new connections had sparked my curiosity and enthusiasm for a time of new learning. An inviting gateway summoned me. All at once, a renewal of hope had me forgetting the childhood fears and confusion in my heart, while it also instilled a greater certainty and confidence that I might somehow conquer that pain inside of me. Whichever was more true, I was being unconsciously driven by my deep-seated need to be understood. My purpose was ignited and my need to feel loved set me forth on a path I could not have imagined.

... I suspect many have walked with me.

The call to a spiritual path is not an invitation to an easy road. Quite the contrary – if there is joy to be found in pain and suffering, you won't find it when you're asleep.

Some desire a simple life while others reject a perceived banality to dive head first into the storms of deeper meaning. Don't be fooled – we all experience both ordinary and extraordinary moments along the way. No matter the path, be assured that the drive to consciously awaken to the Soul's purpose always delivers us nearer to the doorways of seeing into the yet unseen. The good news is that whether you think you're up for the journey or not, you are...simply because you have been gifted this life!

Many times I questioned this for myself. I was so overwhelmed by my emotions to the point of incredulity, yet I couldn't even identify my feelings. I was terribly unqualified to deal with my own sensitivities and emotionality. There was no help at home despite my desperate ways of asking. And as it turned out, venturing into the world was quickly an anxiety-packed ride of chasing shiny things and pleading for the approval of an abandoned child.

Despite feeling disconnected and having to brave my troubles on my own, I learned that we really never do anything alone. The universe holds too much mystery and its guidance takes a myriad of forms. Being open to receiving is most helpful.

While some Lightworkers serve by shining their light of awareness into the darkness, there are some who shine so brilliantly that we are pulled into the greater cause to actively evolve human consciousness. Sometimes they seem like such ordinary people.

Learning was my road and I searched high and low. In a moment of good fortune, I came across a theory through which I could both logically and emotionally value the complex patterns of the apparent and hidden contradictions of all things... *paradox*. It proved very satisfying as I began to make better sense of my world.

I was soon liberated by a growing awareness that every moment was my teacher. It wasn't too much longer before I realised that sitting alone in the dark would actually deliver me to the light. I do believe we are all meant to shine through the darkness in our world.

Life was the greatest teacher guiding me home. My feint pilot light of optimism had inspired me to keep my heart open. What had I been given and what did it really mean for me? I sifted through all my 'stuff' again – the pain, the issues, the emotions. I looked for perspective though I could not have anticipated the answers that would emerge. Despite my excitement, I was cautious that my theoretical friend was only explaining things to my mind; I hoped I would know the truth as it touched my heart.

For each of us, the answer to the question of what we most need is often a paradox. It seems that one of the best presents I ever received was not getting what I wanted. Quite honestly it is still hard for me to fathom: I was a child who wanted to feel the reassurance of unconditional love.

There's always a reason why we don't get what we want, entitled or not. The simple answer is that people can't give you what they don't have; no manner of asking shall provide it.

Although someone cannot give you what they don't have, the choice of not giving it can indeed be *the gift*, as if giving by not giving. This is the first paradox. It would be easy to think this a matter of semantics, but it is far more a matter of perception. When I didn't get what I believed I needed, I was wounded very deeply. I was to learn that this was the gift, a blessing in disguise.

Not leaving out the possibility that when something is not bestowed upon us from one place or person that it may come from another, you may be wondering how to find the gift you have not been given.

When things are not so obvious, it becomes a matter of seeing into the unseen. I reviewed what I knew and what I had come to believe. And I kept my mind focused on that little bit of faith that had told me that everything we need is, in fact, given to us. I held my breath as I took a deliberately deep dive to uncover the truth that would be the key to healing my wound; I had to find my hidden treasure. I mean, really… did I honestly have what was missing?

Looking into your wounds is really unpleasant. It feels like you are having your heart ripped open and everything is on display to the whole world. It is nothing short of vulnerable. Allowing myself every chance to see, I looked, then stared, and with a little time, I saw. Upon deeper reflection I could see why my asking for love was made redundant.

I realise that a theoretical reframing of painful events in our lives is potential trickery for some. My belief systems and the logic I had previously known were all being tested. And though this seemed a reliable way out of the darkness for me, I'm not convinced that I actually believe every possibility I entertained. But where is the answer if not in the question?

So here's another paradox. Along the road, so long as you feel this ungifted thing is still missing, you will likely re-experience your anguish. Sometimes it will show up as a painful witnessing of someone else receiving the exact thing you are wanting. Your torment will be amplified as if you are being denied all over again. What on earth do you have to do to get what you need so you can feel the way you want to feel?

I said before, someone can't give you what they don't have. Paradoxically or otherwise, it is just as true that you can't receive what you already have. The purpose of being the witness is simply to understand why you are reliving your pain of not receiving. You are being awakened to another opportunity to recognise what is already within you. Buried beneath the logical yet unnecessary emotional reactions you may have in the moment of witnessing, know that whatever it is that sits inside the pain of your longing, your gift awaits.

Think about it. How is it possible that not only are you clear about the gift you should have received, but you can describe it in grand detail – how it looks, how and when it shows up in your life, where you are and who you are with when it shows up, and how you feel as a result of its presence? How could you know so much about something you have never had? How could you know the experience of having it, if you had never had it? Perhaps it is that you are not imagining it – perhaps you are remembering it...

Wounds are a special gift. Wounds are not here to punish us, but to release us from the pain we internalised as punishment. Wounds are not here to suggest we are unworthy but to show us that we are not valuing our worth. It is when we uncover the truth buried inside our wounds, and we understand our heart-based message – as if reading the card that comes with the gift – that we can be transformed.

I have broken my own heart so many times over: because I didn't understand; because I chose to believe things that were not true; because I saw my wounds as a reflection of who I was and then used them to continue punishing myself. I saw you abandoning me as my punishment rather than seeing my abandonment as a gift that would teach me independence. Perspective is a beautiful, ever-unfolding thing that reminds us that everything happens for a reason, and all for our highest good.

With my heart closed by hurt, I felt unloved, unacceptable and condemned. I believed this was how you must have been feeling, too; how else could you give that to me! Perhaps you couldn't yet see that you could come to love others through loving yourself.

Let me say that 'tough love' is a betrayal of the heart that has no real reverence for you because the place from which it comes has no reverence for its own heart. It may be called 'love', but tough love does not come from the heart; it is a strategy that mimics learned behaviours from earlier generations when much more about love was assumed, significantly unexpressed, rather less demonstrated and worst of all, quietly overlooked for its deceptions and transgressions.

You know, even if it was true, even for just a moment, that you meant to hurt me, I know it was the pain of your wound that was doing the hurting. I realised long ago that you too had been hurt so as to not know love; and like me, you wanted to feel loved. I know now that through cycles of hurt and pain, what is not love is a call to love. The authentic call to love is sourced from the pain within; from inside our wounds and from deeper within the Soul that is love. Wounds are our clues to what needs most to be healed.

By the grace of a higher power to help you gift it, and through my open heart to receive it, I am grateful for the gift you never gave to me. From you, I learned about the lack of love; because of you, I have come to recognise the many places where love is found. I am sure that if you look, you too, will most surely find it buried in the wounds of your heart.

The story of feeling unloved is a universal story. As my understanding waited patiently for me inside the wounds of my childhood, I am grateful to those wounds as they continue to bring me home. I hold reverence for all I have received as I recognise I am a child of a limitless universe some call God… Love is everywhere and I am love. It is by looking within that we remember who we are and we come home to the light that is love.

As we come to know ourselves in different ways and through different means, our minds and hearts are opening and strangers are sending love to all corners of our global village. The compassionate resonance of new heart connections is real and I suspect this will call many of us to have our hearts broken wide open to be washed by this reverent wave of consciousness.

If we can offer compassion to those who hearts have not yet broken open, if we can share this new-found global wave of acceptance with those not ready to surrender, then we are at least aware that those who struggle to love freely are indeed the ones who do need it the most.

This life is a journey of healing (from the Greek helos, meaning whole) – a journey to wholeness no less. Paradoxically, I see upon reflection that my need was not to be understood, but to understand. By making sense of my world, I made sense of myself. I remain gratefully aware that it is not in spite of the struggle but because of the struggle that I have gained reverence for the path I have forged. Seriously, only I could have imagined my path.

Be invited to know yourself, to embrace all that is you so that you may discover the gift of finding your way home to YOU (Your Own Understanding). It is an opportunity to trade with the universe – to swap fear for love – and to realise you are gifted with all you will ever need.

As I continue to walk this healing journey of awakening, I realise it is really a journey of remembering the truest and most unattached gift of reverence and compassion for myself...

...because that's what coming home is all about.

Stuart appeared, opened the door and entered the room where they had last stood together. A swag of treasures was laid upon the table and Joy heard that familiar voice as it announced, "I'm home." She felt an excited smile enter her heart.

Joy: Oh, yes! I just knew you were coming home, I could feel it. Oh! It's like you never left…

Stuart: Hmmm. Do you remember what you said before I left? Do you remember you said I'd never leave you? You even said it was pretty well guaranteed…

Joy: I do remember. *Oh! I do remember…* we will never be apart, child. No matter where you go, you cannot leave; you are always with me, within me.

Stuart was pleased to see her, too. Joy laughed and tears filled her eyes. She paused in the awareness and then finished...

Joy: Yes. Sometimes I think you are me.

They shared tea and tales as the child reflected joy in every story.

She had kept the light on. And she was home.

Allow your truth, the truth you hold in your heart,
to keep the fire of your courage and your trust well lit.
It will guide you and bring you all the way.

We are, after all, our own Masters.

About the Author: *Robyn M James*

Robyn James is an Energy Healer and Empowerment Coach who graduated with a Degree of Bachelor of Applied Science in Health Education from the University of Canberra (Australia), in 1997. Following two years of tutoring in the same degree, which she absolutely loved, Robyn worked across all levels of the health sector to successfully implement national and state policies and programs for injury prevention, aids education, cancer screening and Aboriginal Health Workforce issues. Despite this purposeful work, an earlier introduction to metaphysical health and illness would remain central to her pursuits in 'alternative health'.

Robyn followed her passion and ventured into learning about mind-body medicine. This area of learning quickly expanded to include consciousness, human behaviour and a deeper pursuit of understanding energy. Today, Robyn holds more than 20 certifications incorporating 10 energy healing modalities.

Back in 2006, it was early days for this developing healer when she established her own healing business, Inside Potential. It was aptly named to signify her profound awareness that at all times we exist within the amazing potentiality of this wondrous universe, while simultaneously being the seed of our own potential essence that we are here to unfold in this lifetime.

While this was an exciting milestone, it would take another year before she would experience that incredible moment of exhilaration as she discovered a deep and profound affinity with Pranic Energy Healing. With specialised experience as an Advanced Pranic Healer for more than seven years now, Robyn has facilitated miraculous healings, received great feedback about the effects of her in-person and distance healings, and skillfully dealt with a range of physical, emotional and mental health issues including the elimination of phobias and addictions. What she loves most about Pranic Energy Healing is that it is a scientifically proven modality of healing, with more than twenty years of research, testing and positive results to its credit. Robyn holds a licence to teach!

As a reflection of her own unfolding journey of healing, Robyn brings together a profound understanding of human behaviour in terms of consciousness, emotions and, as she puts it, a little bit of cereal-box-psychology. A gifted intuitive, her ability to empath-ise allows her the insight and experience of feeling her clients' emotions and physical pain. While this provides a great avenue for guided healing, as a Lightworker, Robyn's goal is to always empower her clients through their healing process.

She offers a unique combination of modalities that are individually tailored to the person's physical and emotional needs, supported with relevant education and the required level of spiritual counselling. Robyn does not claim to heal anyone though she is convinced that amazing things often happen... ready or not!

Robyn's clients praise her ability to hold a beautiful, nurturing space of healing from a place of no judgment; they trust her skills, abilities and insights because they feel supported, and they get results. She laughs that success is when they don't come back!

Although she has many reasons to believe in magic, Robyn is grounded enough to recognise she has been profoundly blessed to have found a way into understanding the power we have to heal. She is grateful to have a well resourced tool kit and for the opportunity to be of service to those who want to create healing in their lives.

By her own experience, Robyn will tell you that the invitation to heal yourself is the invitation (a call, or directive) to know yourself. Based on how she has come to put the pieces together to answer to the deepest wounds in her own life, she will tell you that healing happens when we hold that intention and when we allow ourselves to be served by the insights into our own lives; it is about opening to our own unique possibilities and reconnecting to who we truly are that will set us free. Robyn works in her Healing Studio in Brisbane, Australia. When she is not there, she is out speaking and delivering workshops to groups about healing and how to become more of your authentic self. You are invited to discover and more deeply experience your inside potential through contacting Robyn nationally and internationally for healings, coaching, speaking and more via email, Skype and social media.

Get connected with Robyn via email to insidepotential@gmail.com or via Skype inside.potential and enjoy inspiring and informative updates by visiting Inside Potential on Facebook at https://www.facebook.com/insidepotential or connect and introduce yourself via LinkedIn – au.linkedin.com/in/robynjamesinsidepotential ... and finally, visit the developing website at www.insidepotential.com.au.

Chapter 8

What Do the Bible, Dandelions, a Third Child, and an Ex-Racehorse Know about the Gentle Art of Receiving?

By Elizabeth Anglin

I haven't always been a lucky person.

Well, okay, perhaps that isn't entirely true. I was lucky to be born third in my family, and the second girl, so I learned early about the gentle art of receiving my older sister's hand-me-down clothing. She was five years older, so when I was in elementary school, her cast away clothing that fit me was always just a little bit out of style. But it kept me warm in the winter, and drove away any potential of the dreaded "being at school naked" anxiety dream coming true.

My mother, a penny pincher, and a prodigious knitter, made and gifted me timeless woolen hats and mittens. One could never tell exactly what color they were because she only used scraps of yarn from bigger knitting projects, like baby blankets and afghan throws, but they were still timeless, the way mittens and hats are in Charles Shultz's cartoon illustrations of Charlie Brown, Peppermint Patty, and Marcy, playing in the winter wonderland, building snowmen and ice-skating on the pond. Both activities I enjoyed in abundance, receiving them as gifts of winter in ever-snowy Michigan.

When I grew up, there were things I needed to unlearn as an adult "third child" navigating my way through the larger world. One of them, the first and most important "gentle art" as in the gentle art of receiving…was the gentle art of becoming self-defined. I needed to stop allowing myself to be defined by others, no matter how loving, well-meaning, or protective, they perceived their definitions of me to be. Which leads us to the first life skill necessary in the gentle art of receiving: Be self-defined.

This was a difficult lesson, because as the third child, I wanted to prove myself worthy of the positive attention to my older siblings, by taking an interest in, and becoming proficient at, the things they liked to do and were "good at" doing. So, because my sister wanted to become an actress when she grew up, as soon as I was able to read well enough, I took an interest in her acting by helping her learn lines, playing all the other parts in the plays she had roles in. My older brother was an outdoor guy, good with horses, good with fishing and camping, and good with finding his way in the woods… so I became interested in, and good at, horses, camping, fishing, and finding my way in the woods. He became a National Park Ranger. My sister went on to star in "General Hospital" and other TV shows. I simply became a proficient actor and a proficient outdoorswoman. Probably because my original desire was to secure their attention, not create a greater life for myself by doing what they did.

The next thing I had to overcome on the path to self-definition was growing up in a family of story-tellers. My father was by far the strongest storyteller of the bunch. His "stories" or "definitions" of me always mattered more to me than the stories or definitions of anyone else. Sometimes I would do things I knew he would be interested in simply to hear him tell the story about it later. I was quite heroic and adventurous as a kid, because tales of the "hero" and "adventurer" are the easiest to re-tell, and doing something "heroic" was sure to attract my father's storytelling interest.

Because of this desire to hear stories others told about me, as a young adult, I found myself in a series of monogamous, but heart-breaking, relationships with men. These men naturally stepped into my father's role as "story-teller about me" because I energetically begged them to, and then received their stories hopefully, even when it meant *they* defined *me*. Unfortunately, they often didn't have the parental pride and love my father peppered throughout his stories, and this often meant that they defined me as someone other than who I was.

It wasn't until the last relationship in the series began to end that I realized what I was doing. As the relationship became more and more strained, I listened in horror as my soon to be ex-fiancé told me what I was thinking, feeling, and wanting at any given moment. A communication behavior I at first believed showed me that he noticed me and was thinking about me, and (what joy!) had a story to tell about me, became a relationship prison. He now engaged in full out, no holds barred, mixed martial arts, *defining of me*...my hopes, my dreams, my fears, and my expectations. He believed he was 100 percent accurate and correct in his definition of me. When I tried to explain how his definition of me, (and my hopes, dreams, fears and expectations) was incorrect, I was instigating a fight.

I had allowed him to define me so often and so thoroughly, I could no longer explain myself to him, or be myself with him. There was no "true me" allowed in the relationship. I no longer existed, as myself, for him.

When I did meet with him after the break-up, he would tell me about myself, and I, not being able to get a word in edgewise, would politely listen, nod, pass the spaghetti, and ask if he wanted more wine. Then he would leave, and I would find myself so frustrated I wanted to scream, feeling as if the words he used to define me were a hatchet, used to chop up my soul, like so much dry, brittle, kindling... easily burnable, but unable to maintain long term light and heat.

The saddest part of this lesson was that when our relationship started out, we both wanted, in apparent divine harmony, the same major experiences in life. Of any relationship I had up until that point, I was being my "truest self" with him.

By the time the relationship ended, it was clear that he actually didn't know what he wanted, and that at the beginning of the relationship, he found my dreams as good as any he might have had for himself… and so there we were, me being my true self, dreaming my true dreams, and him pretending to be dreaming the same dreams, and later, him defining me as someone I wasn't, because he no longer wanted to pretend to be dreaming the same dreams I dreamed.

When the relationship was over, I had to accept that the dreams I had "with him" were my own dreams, dreams from my "true self" and that he had no power to keep me from realizing and experiencing them.

Which leads us to the second life skill necessary in the gentle art of receiving: Be independent.

By learning to be steadfastly self-defined, you set yourself up to receive a life that is uniquely created to fit you… a life you truly want. Allowing yourself to be defined by others sets you up to receive a life that makes *you* fit *them*…or disempowers you. I don't know about you, but I'm like one of those expanding dinosaur spongy toys. You know the toys that expand when you put them in water? Eventually I just won't fit any box someone else tries to make me fit in, because I have the energy and the nature to expand beyond it.

Similarly, being independent, and not waiting for someone else to "provide your life for you" or "be with you" while you pursue and receive the life you want, leaves your best life an open path to your door. There is no conflicting energy to stop you from pursuing making the life you truly want, or stop the universal mailman from delivering your "Hey, cool, look... this is my life!" straight to you.

Does this mean you need to be alone to receive the life you want? Well, no. It just means you need to be honest about who you are, and seek to be with someone who is equally as honest about who they are... and then, if your desires are not completely identical, don't worry about it or judge each other...be honest about it, and support each other in your dreams and desires as much as you can. However, if your desires for a certain kind of life are completely identical, shout "Halleluiah!" and be thankful that you can work so easily together on creating the conditions for receiving the same experiences.

Start your path to receiving with self-definition, add in honesty about that self-definition, and then to take responsibility for yourself with independence. No matter who is with you, or who is around you, being independent also means you are not blaming anyone else for what you are not receiving, or doing, with your life.

Life skill number three in the gentle art of receiving: "Just go straight. Don't run around in circles."

This wisdom comes straight from the horse's mouth....the ex-racehorse's mouth. When you have become self-defined, when you have explored what you truly want in life and have a good visualization of it, when you are basically independent, you might still trip yourself up on the path to receiving with a compulsive desire to "run around in circles doing for other people."

I spent a few years doing this because I was afraid of "the unknown" - what would happen if I truly "went for" what I wanted in my life? It took my rescued ex-racehorse, TNT, a grandson of Northern Dancer and Diplomat Way (both won "Horse of the Year" awards) to lay it down for me. When asked, he dished out succinct and timely tough love, calling me out on my procrastinating, fearful, behavior.

"Just go straight, don't run around in circles. Just go straight. Even when you can't see a thing but the butts in front of you and the mud in your eyes, trust that God will remove these obstacles when you are ready to move forward."

As I heard his words in my head, I saw a scene he laid out for me, visually, mentally, and emotionally. It was of him, breaking at the back of the pack of horses on a muddy race day. His face was covered with mud, and the rumps of the horses ahead of him heaved up and down, covered with thick mud, roiling like brown waves in a brown ocean, blocking his path to the front. He had all the energy and power he needed to win the race. His goal, the thing he really wanted to experience, was winning the race... and he didn't blame the other horses for being in his way for a moment, he didn't blame God for making the track muddy, he took complete responsibility for himself. He waited, and *trusted,* that the opening he needed, the opening that would lead to winning the race…was going to appear. He also ran straight for the finish line… he didn't pretend he had something else more important to do before he got there!

And this leads us to the fourth life skill in the gentle art of receiving: "Be willing to move."

A good friend of mine calls this skill, "You can't get to America by staying in England."

I like to think of it as "The Dandelion" skill.

Have you ever noticed that dandelions can grow almost anywhere? As a child, did you ever hold up a dandelion that had turned to seed, and then blow on it? Do you remember how satisfying it felt to watch the seeds take flight in the wind, moving to where good soil, light and water would find them?

I believe the only reason people refuse to move toward their good, the life they desire to receive, experience, and grow through, is because of fear of the unknown. If this is where you are stuck on your path of receiving, consider adopting the courage of a dandelion seed. It doesn't know everything about where it will land and plant itself, but it does "trust" that it will land somewhere good, somewhere it can grow.

The other thing the dandelion does not do, is to try to control, or judge what goes on in the field around it. It simply moves to where it can grow, and it lets other plants, flowers, animals, and people, do the same.

And this leads us to the fifth, and final life skill in the gentle art of receiving: "Be effortless."

If a dandelion doesn't convince you that you are divinely designed to receive what you need, as well as what you want, effortlessly, then consider the lilies of the field… or as the Bible says in Matthew 6:25-34:

"Therefore I tell you, do not be anxious about your life, what you will eat or what you will drink, nor about your body, what you will put on. Is not life more than food, and the body more than clothing? Look at the birds of the air: they neither sow nor reap nor gather into barns, and yet your heavenly Father feeds them. Are you not of more value than they? And which of you by being anxious can add a single hour to his span of life? And why are you anxious about clothing? Consider the lilies of the field, how they grow: they neither toil nor spin, yet I tell you, even Solomon in all his glory was not arrayed like one of these."

I especially like the part about "neither sow, nor reap, nor gather into barns" – it's so much WORK to collect stuff… and what does it get you in the long run? I know people who spend most of their time simply managing the over-abundance of things they own, and then not being able to move toward the things they would truly like to receive because they are terrified that they will lose what they already have, even when what they already have is not what they really want (or ever wanted) to receive!

The key here is truly trusting in the universe, and practicing "effortlessness." If there is a life experience, or gift, or situation that you truly want to receive, something you as your true self incarnated on earth to be, do and have... if you leave room for it, and then don't obsess about it anxiously, it will come to you... in the perfect way at the perfect time.

Before it does, there is no need to (anxiously) fill up your closets with clothes you don't really want to wear, and experiences you don't really want to have. Make room. Let the things that you don't want, and never wanted...go.

And then don't make the effort to collect more of them.

When you leave yourself open for receiving what you really want, the universe will easily, and effortlessly, begin to send it to you.

ABOUT THE AUTHOR: *ELIZABETH ANGLIN*

Elizabeth Anglin is an Animal Communicator, Spirit Medium, and Psychic. When she was a child she wanted to communicate with animals, like Dr. Doolittle. She tried for months, then years, crying herself to sleep at night because she couldn't manage to talk to animals in the way she wanted to. When she was 28, the skill came to her, effortlessly, years after she stopped trying.

Elizabeth also believed when she was young, that she was going to discover something new and unusual about the world, and be involved in scientific research around this unusual thing. She thought it had to do with finding aliens, but she wasn't sure. At the age of 24, she was visited by aliens in her apartment, and soon after began researching her alien related experiences with Dr. John E. Mack, at Harvard University, speaking about her experiences at both MIT and Harvard.

Afterwards, Elizabeth dreamed of moving to the Rocky Mountains and living on a ranch with horses, surrounded by nature and wild animals. Afraid of moving away from her friends, her job, and everything else she had become accustomed to, she procrastinated and didn't pursue her dream. Even when her own horse told her she needed to move, convincingly, she procrastinated. Finally, all of her family members in spirit showed up for a spirit medium sitting and said "Listen, you need to move to the Rocky Mountains, and by this date, so get on it." She moved on the exact date her family members in spirit gave her, and within four years of the move, found herself living on a high mountain ranch, with her horses, surrounded by nature and wild animals.

Elizabeth is available for private sessions through http://www.elizabethanglin.com.

Her memoir, "Experience: Memoirs of an Abducted Childhood" can be explored at http://www.experiencememoirs.com.

Chapter 9

Balancing the Chi of Earth: A Feng Shui Perspective on Giving and Receiving

By Diane Hiller

As a Psychic Medium, Feng Shui expert, and Licensed Psychotherapist, I have a perspective that weaves the wisdom of the Ancient masters with today's spirit. I have dedicated my life to the understanding of the ancient knowledge and I am joyful today to share with you how you may be able to open to a greater state of receiving taking into account the practices and beliefs behind Feng Shui, Yin Yang, and the system of the five elements. Enjoy!

I stumbled across Feng Shui through synchronicity in the years 2000 to 2001. I had just purchased a new home, leaving the one I had lived in for 20 years after a major life change. I was at a loss in the use of color, and feeling at a loss in general, when I happened upon a new friend that I had met at a family wedding. Though I had been on a spiritual path for over a decade, I had not yet found the system or philosophy that, in my mind, would pull it all together, or which seemed to resonate. My newfound friend, who was an artist, gave me a book on Feng Shui. My house was totally torn apart. I left it that way for four months while I read as much as I could. I went out and bought four more books. It then took me four more months just to figure out where to place the Bagua map! I began to work with color in ways I never had before, to understand the energy of the colors. I activated my entire home by color. It took years. Still I felt there was more to learn, there always is, but here I was certain that I wanted to commit the time and energy.

I then started to seek out more information about certification programs. I liked the way Feng Shui was interrelated with the I Ching, how the Baguas actually were derived from its text, philosophy and deeply profound wisdom. I found that although Feng Shui was about color and energy, it was far more comprehensive than I would have ever imagined. Here was a system of ancient knowledge that was handed down only from mentor to student. One that looked at life in a certain way, that showed me how the outer circumstances, in all ways, were a reflection of inner thought and my own deep psychological and spiritual interior.

I saw this as win/win. I could learn a new profession and gain more spiritual knowledge, yet at the same time, work on myself as a spiritual being. I would emerge with a new knowledge base, more awake and aware. Throughout those three years (which took every ounce of my free time, vacation days and personal time and some of it unpaid time), I was deeply transformed in ways unimaginable to me now. I share with you some of the principles that helped me to get unstuck. I show you how I was able to gain balance, and to learn to look at life through a more expansive and interconnected lens. These are powerful techniques and they will work. If you put in the intention and work, you will see the results. If you are stuck, exhausted from over giving, or loving too much, and not getting your needs met, it is my hope that these tools will be of help to you on your journey.

From a Feng Shui perspective, giving and receiving is addressed in several different concepts. One is the Yin and the Yang. The other concept in the Black Sect Tibetan Buddhist School has to do with the Five Element System, although both are interrelated. Chi is the energy or life force present in all things and beings. Here we look at imbalances with giving and receiving in terms of the five elements: water, wood, fire, earth, and metal.

Earth chi is specifically the Chi of giving and receiving. Its relative presence or absence in your energetic system will manifest in your life along the continuum of selfishness versus selflessness. In its extreme, it can manifest as being too egocentric or feeling like a doormat. Earth Chi can be the most complex of elements. It is the most important element to adjust or have in balance, as it is connected to the Yin and Yang and the Central position of the Feng Shui Bagua known as the Tai Chi, from which *all that is* arises. It is connected to the spleen and the stomach. Its taste is sweet. It is the sound of singing and the color associated with this energy is yellow or earth tones. It is the element that represents how we take care of others and ourselves. How we give and how we receive, and how we make our boundaries.

When a person has a personal Four Pillars chart done in Chinese Astrology, the chart will show the exact numerical value of each element in his or her own personal system. Those with giving and receiving issues will have an over-abundance numerically of earth chi. Many women, plus those in the helping profession, light workers and other givers, will be found to have an earth chi imbalance. This core dynamic is also found in those who were raised in very dysfunctional households with the dynamic of subtle or overt abuse. Knowing that there is a problem is the first step in making adjustments. Getting this element back in to balance is crucial for all of us. The risk inherent in not doing so can lead to poor communication, anger, frustration, burnout and physical illness.

Many people wonder why they are thinking and doing and trying so hard to manifest something, and yet it is not forth coming. I have observed recurrent themes running though this central issue. I do not believe that manifestation is quite as simple as it has been made out to be in the popular media. Thinking simply does not make it so. I believe the key lies within our own internal dialogue and subconscious belief systems. To balance the chi of earth there are specific Feng Shui rituals (that are beyond the scope of this chapter) that you can use. However, what they do in essence is to bring into your conscious awareness that which has been hidden from view. While these rituals are helpful you can also simply commit each day noticing and stating your intent to the universe. Each morning say out loud to the universe and your guides "Show me where my earth chi is out of balance." Make a minimum of a 27, 36, or 45-day commitment. The time commitment must add up to nine and nine is the number of completion in Feng Shui.

To further demonstrate your commitment to significant change you can also do a well known Feng Shui ritual which involves moving 27 items that have not been moved in over a year's time at your place of residence. For example: you can move a picture from one place to another or your dresser by even a quarter of an inch. Any item counts, as long as it is moved. Doing so breaks up stagnant chi and also shows your readiness for change. Now would also be a good time to do a space clearing ritual to remove negative chi such as burning White Sage or Chen Pi comprised of dried orange peels that can be found in Chinese Medicine stores. To do this clearing, you cut and place nine round circles of a store bought orange in the center of a white plate and surround them by nine pieces of Chen Pi, and walk throughout the house visualizing that bad energy has left. In our tradition we chant the universal mantra Om Ma Ni Pad Me Hum. Use whatever cleansing ritual speaks to you.

Now is a time for being *very aware* of your own self and your interactions with others. Keep a journal, of what makes you feel good and, well, not so good. Where do you consistently give and get nothing back? Who makes you feel exhausted and worn out? Where is the pattern of imbalance at home, work, in your friendships and love life? You need not act yet, just pay close attention to these issues and keep a journal of the patterns. Pay close attention to your "gut feelings," this is, as you recall, connected to your spleen and stomach. Follow your internal compass and intuition and learn to trust yourself and your feelings.

After you have become your own life detective, with the goal of inner adjustment, you will see the patterns that need to be changed. You may recognize patterns like when and where you said yes when you really meant no; when you over-gave and got nothing in return; when you felt tapped out and still did more; or when you recognized a friendship had become unhealthy. You will begin to see where your own life is not in order and neglected because you spent too much time on other's needs. You will find when and where you gave up pieces of yourself to get love or stay in a relationship. This process is not for the faint of heart, yet staying stuck is just as, if not, more painful. Many of us want changes yet are afraid of the unknown or to rock the boat. Many know they need to change and will engage the process. Some will have it forced upon them. I believe those of you seeking change in this area will somehow find this book and this chapter will come into your hands.

Once you call upon the forces of the universe for internal change and commit to it, it will come. After all, you may have been trying to get others to change, finding your efforts unsuccessful and expending huge amount of emotional energy doing so. Now you can change, and you can start right now this very minute. For example, the phone rings, you are tired. You know on the other end is a friend that you find draining, you always take their call and then after are really exhausted and resentful. Next time the call comes, you just don't answer. When you are ready you will engage the person and say something along the lines of, "I value our friendship but more and more I find myself exhausted after our talks, I do not feel supported or that there is a give and take, are you willing to work on this issue?" The person may be surprised or they may get angry. They may not want to change the pattern of venting on you and feeling relieved. If so, then you have a decision to make. You can limit your call time, or you can decide this person is toxic and can no longer be with the new person you are becoming. You want a mutually supportive and loving connection, a win/win for everyone. With family this is a bit harder, you may simply need to set stronger boundaries and not get into the "hot topics" that you know will push your buttons.

When one decides to work intensively on the issue of giving and receiving; and perhaps setting new boundaries and expectations for oneself and others; issues tend to come to a head rather quickly. It may feel that you are getting hit in all directions.

You will know change is happening because it will be the same issue at home, at work, with your friends, your lover, and so on. Now that you have taken a good look and do not like what you see, you will begin to act or respond differently to make changes. Outer events and circumstances may change in ways you do not initially see as helpful, or internal conflict may begin, friends may leave, your new-found independence may not work for some who are used to you carrying more that your share. People may choose to leave your life or you may choose to let them go. At this point people may come in and out your life. Life may feel unstable. Chaos always precedes order and true change cannot occur without it. The key here is to getting in touch with you. Touch your true genuine self. Remember to remind yourself that you do not need to do this all at once. You can go slow and tackle one area at a time. Once you begin to feel more empowered, and you will, you can move on to the next issue. The empowered person makes choices out of love, self-love and love for those around them. You can learn how to respond rather that react. Just slow down your own process.

The key is to focus on your own internal messages. Support yourself while making these changes. You may feel selfish and guilty. After all, these patterns have been here for some time, and it will take some time to shift them.

There are things you can do to support yourself in loving ways while you make changes. Eat well, and get enough rest. Meditate. Take long hot baths. Surround yourself with the color yellow. Wear yellow clothes and eat yellow foods.

Find some yellow citrine and wear it as jewelry. Go for a massage. Increase your physical activity when you feel anger. Write out your feelings and burn them, do not act in anger, and expect it to arise. Prepare for it. This is not about what other people do or not do, it is about you what you allow, nor longer allow, and how you are going to do choose to do things differently.

You are working with the Tai Chi, so pay attention to what is in the Tai Chi or direct center of your home. This is a good time to fill that space with earth elements, flowers in water, bowls of fruit, stones in water with Bamboo, whatever calls to you that is of the earth.

Chanting specific mantras may also help you to shift and feel more empowered or also help to soften your heart. For empowerment I like the Green Tara Mantra, she represents the mother of liberation, enlightened activity in thought, speech and action, and helps to deliver us from the three spiritual dangers of greed, hated and delusion believed to be at the root cause of all suffering. Her mantra is Om Tare Tu Tare Ture Svaha.

Often too in this tradition one may "Borrow the Buddha's Chi" by using a mantra from the Heart Sutra "Gate Para Gate, Para Sum Gate Bodhi Svaha." One does this by placing your hand under your heart left over right and chanting (again in rounds of nine) the above mantra. This mantra translates to mean, gone, gone, completely gone and crossed over to the enlightened state. It helps to calm the mind and heart in times of distress.

Perhaps it is best to close now with the concept of surrendered action. While engaged in this intention to be more open to receive, one may acknowledge our own blocks and behaviors that have been unskillful at best and harmful to ourselves at their worst. You are now taking action though speech and deed that is based on love of self and others and you surrender the outcome to the highest good of all. This is very different from taking action to gain an outcome or to force change. You are now acting worth a purpose to open yourself to more love, to only situations that are reciprocal in nature, to mutually beneficial scenarios. Trust yourself, the process, God, and the universe. Act with kindness and watch your life begin to transform.

ABOUT THE AUTHOR: *DIANE HILLER*

Diane Hiller is a Psychic Medium, Medical Intuitive, Psychotherapist and Certified Feng Shui Master and bestselling author. She is an innovative expert in the field of metaphysics and is widely recognized in her field. She is a former nurse and Phi Beta Kappa receiving both her undergraduate degree in Psychology and Master's in Clinical Social Work at The University of Connecticut. Diane has extensively studied both Buddhism and Shamanism and received certification as a Black Sect Tibetan Buddhist Feng Shui Master ™. This professional training program was originally formed at the request and under the guidance the late His

Holiness Professor Thomas Lin Yun, a world-renowned expert in Feng Shui. She is a member of the International Feng Shui Guild.

She has been featured in The Top 100 Psychic and Astrologers in America by Paulette Cooper and Paul Noble, in the 2015 Best Psychics Mediums and Lightworkers in the United States, by Maximillian de Lafayette, as well as The National and International Rank of The World's Best Lightworkers 2014-2015 by Maximillian de Lafayette. She was ranked internationally by popular vote as within the top 10 as a Psychic, Psychic Medium, Feng Shui Master and Life Coach.

Diane's psychic gifts were evident at the age of nine. They fully awakened during her personal healing journey, through the study of shamanism and chakra journeywork, then following two very powerful kundalini openings. She is founder and owner of Elemental Empowerments, LLC, in Litchfield, Connecticut and combines the arts of Mediumship, Psychotherapy, Feng Shui, and spiritual life coaching in her professional practice. Diane's educational background and skills give her insight and understanding of your life challenges and her spiritual toolbox is full of abilities to work with you on numerous energetic levels. It is an honor and privilege for Diane to be of service to you. Diane reads locally in her Litchfield office and does phone readings both in the USA and Internationally. Her contact information is as follows:

Phone (860) 601-1263
Email: dianehiller@optonline.net
Website: www.ElementalEmpowerments.com
Facebook: https://www.facebook.com/DianeHillerPsychicMedium?ref=hl

Chapter 10

The Gift

By Josie Blaine

Think of the best gift you ever received. Your mind may drift back to Christmas mornings of your childhood, wading in waist-deep wrapping paper as Mom and Aunt Bonnie rush around the kitchen to coordinate the timing of everything going into and coming out of the oven. Was it the dollhouse with the elevator on a string? Remember the year you finally were tall enough to ride a bike?

The evolution of the doll is not only representative of the age of the receiver, but technology and society as well. Babies snuggle stuffed animals, pre-kindergarten children might get a baby doll, and then when Barbie comes screeching up the street in her pink convertible, things are never the same. Barbie has more clothes, shoes, purses, the horses, the Townhouse, and then along came Ken and Skipper with all of their stuff. Barbie needs all of those houses.

How did the years go so fast? We wonder, uncurling tissue and years-old crumpled newspaper, wrapped around delicate Christmas ornaments that we just must organize and perhaps downsize. I think my family has even sold two Barbie Dream Houses in the process of getting Mom and Dad settled in the retirement house.

There is only one Christopher Radko ornament in this entire 35x60-ft shop. It's' glassblown, glittery presence brings the hustle and bustle to a short pause as Mom and I look at each other, wondering from whence this came, knowing neither of us collects these, and I tell her that someone out on eBay will be happy to add it to their collection. We have way too many bows and garlands, but we can send them to the troops overseas, and brighten up their Christmas.

This is the year Mom gives me about a third of her snow village. She turns the crank on one of the miniature glass buildings and sets it back down, as we box up the others, which I will take home for the first time.

Indeed, it is A Small World after all, the music box house dings along daintily. These are happy tears, and we both know it. The house itself came from Great Uncle George, and he was a great uncle, that George. He was the Santa Claus of the family. Every cousin, aunt and uncle will say the same thing. My Uncle George had been in the army. He was a well-known celebrity as the milkman in our small town. He took the cartons of milk to the school for the children, and restocked the refrigerators of every housewife for 30 years, in an era when people did not lock their doors.

In his later years, he would rake leaves for neighbors, and if it looked like rain, Uncle George might gather laundry off of the clothesline for the lady down the street. By the time Uncle George died, the younger generation in the area didn't know his last name. But they knew George the Milkman. May we all live in a manner so that when we die, people only know us by our kindness. Now and then, I can hear his laughter. Now and then, I find a Christmas card with his handwriting and five dollars in it.

"Use the money for something you want."

These are happy tears.

Receiving a compliment, finding five bucks, realizing we awoke 20 minutes early are all energizing. They are the instigators to what could become winning days. A compliment becomes a smile, a smile turns into more confidence, which eventually garners a raise and a promotion.

Found money may inspire you to buy coffee for the car behind you in the drive-thru. Soon, the line of cars paying it forward reaches into the dozens and the random act of kindness shows up on the news. Look what you have started! Each recipient of kindness feels, in some way, compelled to go forth and give, sending forth a ripple effect of loving proportions, and soon, the world is shivering in joy.

Twenty more minutes in the morning before work might help us all accomplish those resolutions we made at the outset of the New Year.

I could pull that yoga mat out from behind the sofa, unroll it and get Downfacing Dog To Business. I could blow the dust off of my Tai Bo tapes. I could invest in a new water filtration device for my kitchen sink, so I have no excuse not to drench my body with eight, eight-ounce glasses of fresh, clean hydration every day. My skin will thank me so much for all that water, my skin will no doubt march me right to the facialist as a reward on Valentine's Day for being such a sweetheart to my body.

Yeah, baby! I have earned that iced short schitzo skinny mango cappuccino with wings! There was a $10 bill hiding in the Yoga Basics DVD case, and I just now recall that my past self put it there as a gift to my future self. I suppose you could look at it as a reward, if ever I ventured back into the foray of the living room workout. It only makes sense to do what comes naturally and hit the drive-thru, buying a treat for the car behind me. Perhaps it will energize their world.

And the beat goes on.

Nearly two decades ago, a young woman living several hours away from Mom and Dad, and weeks away from Christmas was hanging her Advent Calendar. The days ahead seemed to be filled less with the burgeoning holiday cheer and were jam-packed full of stress and worry. How could it be different?

One dog changed the world. On the drive home from work

after a bad day, Rindy paid the toll for the car behind her on a whim.

It is that moment when you can almost hear Clarence the Angel offering his adage, "Every time a bell rings, an angel gets his wings."

Now it felt like Christmas, Rindy thought. She could kick off her holiday season by doing something nice for someone else. It would be a random act of kindness, or a senseless act of beauty. And, having been a cheerleader and always a natural people person, she would get her friends in on it, too.

Of course it is fun to receive the free coffee in the drive-thru line, but in giving there is also tremendous energy and blessing. God does love a cheerful giver, and I'm sure He laughs when He sees people getting such joy out of giving!

It spread like wildfire locally by phone and email. The next year, Rindy's Random Acts of Kindness Day was coming up, and she would not let anyone within her reach and whisper forget that December First was special. Pay the toll or the coffee bill for the car behind you, or pick up the tab for an unsuspecting diner at a restaurant. Laundry soap and tokens at a Laundromat go a long way toward gifting someone with lasting hope. We all feel better, happier, and more energetic when we are clean.

Do-gooders conduct meetings, share power brunches, and

local civic groups gather on how they will go forth and make Random Acts of Kindness Day better than last year. It has spread all over the Midwest, then throughout the country, and when social media came along, there was no stopping the senseless giving. Some families take hot chocolate and food to the homeless, and businesses have given their employees sums of money expressly to use in paying it forward.

One year, Rindy found a stray dog running on Interstate 94. It was then that she received her Pet Mom Superpowers. She shut down both east and westbound traffic running after him (whoops!). She managed to corral the stray animal, but the number on the dog's tag was disconnected, so she could not find the owner. Rindy fed the dog, brought him to the vet, then called local bars. A bar owner knew the dog and its owner! They called him. The dog's owner suffered from a childhood disease and couldn't drive. So, the dog stayed with me that night, after she went and got him a new collar, leash and dog tag with the correct phone number!! The next morning Rindy drove the dog back to its owner. He tried to pay her, but she would not hear of it.

What is the best gift you have ever received? Has your pet changed your world? That random, once-lost and confused dog, who thought he was a runaway and a stray, has done good for countless lives everywhere.

Winston Churchill told us, "We make a living by what we get. We make a life by what we give."

It is truly more blessed to give than to receive, because the giver has the joy of planning a gift, be it monetary, physical, or spiritual, and waiting for the recipient's reaction. Later, if the gifts are welcomed and received with the right spirit, each gift manifests itself out into the world, growing greater and more powerful for good. Have you ever thrown a surprise party? Random Acts of Kindness are like mini surprise parties that require no cake (but cake is definitely an option!), no stumbling around in the dark, and no creative white lies. Just show up and pay it forward! See what happens when that wonderful, out-of-the-ordinary feeling is passed on. Chances are, you have caused someone to do something nice for someone else. Hopefully, human nature will ensue, and they will happily share their good fortune, in word and deed. The world is not ending. Don't believe the images on television. We can set off a chain reaction of positive giving and receiving that will shudder the earth in her revolution. Just do something to make it better. Best friends will outdo one another with kindness. Treat the world as you would your best friend, and the world will be fine.

Parents will spend all of their lives giving their children gifts like integrity, foundational belief systems, and a work ethic. They are difficult to wrap up and put under the tree, but if they are received well, a beautiful legacy is carried on. What kind of world do you envision?

"I would maintain that thanks are the highest form of thought, and gratitude is doubled by wonder." -- G.K. Chesterton

In the Bible, Jesus encountered a leper colony on the road to Jerusalem. The people were excluded from their families and society, forced to live away from town, and they had formed unit because of their grievous medical condition. They were humiliated and in misery. As travelers approached, they had to warn, "Unclean! Unclean!"

They had been living, cut off from society for so long, they were beside themselves with disbelief and joy when Jesus came past their meager encampment. He told them to go on their way. Their faith had made them well. What a thought process, to go from wasting away to nothing, and being told you are well? From nothing to having everything! What a gift! Jesus healed all 10 lepers, and they ran toward Jerusalem, back to their families and friends. Only one, a Samaritan, already an outcast by nationality before he was ever a leper, turned back to give thanks.

ABOUT THE AUTHOR: *JOSIE BLAINE*

Josie Blaine's great grandpa worked on the railroad. Generations later, Josie grew up playing on the railroad tracks all summer long in North Dakota. She listened to the trains carry coal all night long. Grandma would keep count of the coal cars, calculating the success of the state.

As most young people did in those days,

the North Dakota State University Communications double major hit the interstate, heading south the day after her college graduation. The military kid and radio gypsy has lived in almost every corner of the United States, writing for broadcast, writing for print, and trying out practically every facet of the career of sales/ marketing/communications major should. She had a cat. When the cat died, she bought a house and got a dog.

Understanding that mom was right, and there truly is no place like home, Josie sold her house and followed the railroad back to North Dakota. Here, she could write about her own glowing histories, the rumbling trains across the fresh prairies, and her beloved North Dakota, at the side of Grandma's rocking chair. These days, Josie reports to Grandma on the number of oil cars passing just outside the nursing home, on the tracks that brought the family here so long ago.

Josie loves God, her family, America, The Bison, and coffee. She is the author of the books *Something About Sophia* and *Nowhere, Everywhere*. Her writing appears in local publications.

(Photo by Crown of Laurels Photography, Bismarck, ND)

Chapter 11

What if the Shift into Having Money was Easier?

By Lori Anzini

What if the shift into having money was easier? What if you could receive your own greatness? What if having and receiving was in connection to joy, clarity, focus and intention?

"The amplification of my manifestation has surpassed my willingness to grab it by its horns."

I woke up with those words in my head this morning. This happens to me. A lot. For some reason, my brain and my identity separate into two different characters. The one that says I need this for my own pleasure, and the other that says this is your path of the true nature. It scares me. I don't like it sometimes, but then, when I fully grasp what has just happened, I let go and just say "thy will be done".

This wasn't me several years ago. My identity was different. I was a wife, a career woman, a grandmother, and even a sassy politician. That was me, all caught up in the external race to grab the golden ring, to be in control. It was never for money, but it seemed to come with the race. The money was debt, the money was abundance, the money was joy, and then the money was "just getting by."

Circumstances can change quickly with a snap of the fingers, especially with the death of a spouse. No…you can't measure a divorce with that, it is not even close to comparison. Divorce can be a choice, death is not.

Making plans with a man for over 36 years came easy for me. He let that happen. I was the planner, I was the goal achiever, and he knew that from the beginning. He even told me one time, when we were debating about having a sliding glass door being installed in our bedroom, that my focus on a project scared him. He told me that whenever I visualized a new project, he would cringe. He was always reluctant to change things up, while me – I was moving that furniture around every month or two in order to satisfy my craving for change. If the issue was money, I managed to maneuver priorities so that the glass door went in.

So what has changed since he died? What does this have to say about anything about energy received? I know that energy comes in two forms: the negative and the positive. Proven studies have shown that the human brain does change with positive thinking. I look at it two ways: The energy of his death was most certainly negative. A loss, a yearning, and the grief. We all get it from time to time, it's part of being human. Then there was the positive energy of rebuilding myself into the woman I was before he and I married so long before.

A significant shift came to me with his death. First was the loss of my identity. Then, I realized that it wasn't my identity, I was here all along. It was my loss of joy. The planner in me decided to pull up my "big girl" panties and change it. I started off in baby steps. I sat down with a dry-erase board and started writing to me, "You are Happy". I would stare at the words, close my eyes, open them and then erase the words. I would immediately write "YOU are worthy". Then stare at it, close my eyes, open them, then erase them. Immediately writing down, "You are loved." Then I would repeat the exercise with those phrases, one after another.

It did this each day for about 10 minutes. That's all it took to bring my emotional scale up. After doing that for several days, I realized that my "happy factor" was a whole lot better. I saw a future for me, just me, and it wasn't loneliness, unworthiness, or unhappiness.

Something shifted in me immediately. I started walking, not just a stroll, but a strut. It made me feel better each day I did this. My energy perked up with the exercise, of course, but those positive writing exercises helped pull it all together. This practice also changed my physical body and my mental clarity. After months of practicing these small exercises, I changed it up again.

I added daily meditation. I know, I know, good grief... another one of those people! But it worked. I started to believe that the thoughts of what I would do with my life from that point forward was to do just one thing....to seek joy. I also set my intentions to find it in others and appreciate and observe how each day is just a divine gift. Observing the joy of others made me feel good, it made me feel whole again. Think about just watching little children playing on a playground.

Opportunities started to pop up. A trip to China with a group of women became possible. It was nowhere on my bucket list. But I said yes. I made new friends, I saw places that I had only read about (try the Terra Cotta Warriors) I know my husband was there checking it all out with me.

Then there was a cruise on the Mexican Riviera, and then the bucket list trip of a lifetime, a cruise to New Zealand and Australia. It was interesting how my monetary stability was gradually going down. Somewhere in there, I managed to pull together enough money to buy a house for myself. I had never done that before. I was in this lovely, but sad house, a benefit from someone else's misfortune, but now I was no longer throwing money away on rent.

I got intentionally lucky. I had a lovely man step into my life just about the time I bought that sad little house. The house wasn't sad anymore, and neither was I. He moved in and lightened the load with spiritual energy. The kind I had been seeking for decades but didn't feel I was worthy of and was doubtful I would ever have again.

With his creative musical talent and long-time experience of meditating, he was the validation I needed that I could continue to grow, to experience new things, to travel in freedom, and to express my thoughts and words into writing. I felt free! That creativity was there within me right along, digging and gnawing at me for a very long time, but never expressed. I felt the joy of the freedom that I could finally be myself. The energy continued to flow upwards.

I got creative, because I really, really wanted to go to New Zealand and Australia on a cruise. It was something my husband and I had always wanted to do. My creative juices kicked into gear. How was I going to be able to find the money to take that cruise? I made the decision to rent that house my husband and I had built seven years prior, out in the Northern California remote areas of Humboldt County. It was just sitting there empty of people. I only managed to get to it a few times a year. With some talk with family members that lived near it, and with their approval, I was able to rent it, allowing money to flow into my escrow of travel, and repairing the sad state of the house I had just purchased.

I experienced that decision with a lot negative energy, because I allowed my adult children to send it to me, sending me into a quagmire of doubt, depression, and isolation. I was removed from their lives, but I had the wonderful fortune of my sister-in-law, and that new man. They supported me emotionally, gently reminding me that this was my "me" time.

I went on the cruise and made many new friends, all free and positive thinkers. I was in a circle of people that I could relate to, have dialogue about finding joy, and sharing ways to discourage negative thoughts.

I also did an important task. I took a little of my husband's ashes with me, and scattered them in Doubtful Sound. It was an important tribute to his life-long scientific belief that there is no God, no single-sourced answered of why humanity exists, but his most agnostic belief was "there must be something". It was perfect and I know he was there with me, enjoying the scenic view of the Sound and the mountains surrounding the beauty of the water. The minute I scattered those ashes, I knew that somewhere along this rocky path I journeyed, I had healed. It wasn't an easy path; it was one with misgivings, doubts, and self-recriminations. But I also have learned that when we go through these upheavals, we become stronger and resilient.

Upon my return from that wonderful trip, I finally unleashed the words I needed to write about the grief and the journey I was following. This helped me heal, but it also helped my children understand that I was not just their mother, but a human being with interests other than being a wife, a politician, a mother, and a grand-mother. I needed to thrive.

The book that I had been "journaling" for four years was published: *Escaping the Jaws of Life: A Widow's Journey to Happiness.* It helped others realize that when grief hits you, the journey will be tumultuous and can throw you into an imbalanced state of woe.

I now continue my journey as a writer, an artist, and a joy seeker. With inspired hope. When I inspire, I feel the energy soaring in me. I'm not just receiving that energy, I am reflecting it onto others and giving it to them.

So with this renewed "me", I have experienced so many new outlets of fun and joy. It's not coming in the form of money, it's coming in the form of growth. Since my trip to New Zealand and Australia, I have since gone another cruise to Italy, Greece, and Turkey. I was again surrounded by some of those new friends from cruises before. Surrounded by inspired joy seekers. A reflection of what I truly wanted and perhaps had become.

My adult children are starting to understand that I am a human, not just a mother. I have two more grand-daughters since my husband's death. I have a continued understanding with the new man in my life, that I am more important than anyone else. He worships himself in the same way. The spiritual practice of meditation is much stronger in him, and I am easily deluded into my obsessive-compulsive "got to be perfect" behavior. He sees through that and gently reminds me that my energy is perfect the way it is. We both understand through our own trials with money, debt, and abundance that everything is working out the way it is supposed to.

Today, I'm celebrating the fact that I sold the little house I bought five years ago. I have done a stunning job of acquiring enough money from the sale to move very close to my son and his family and become a full-fledged grandmother. A grandmother, much like the ones I'm writing about, but with a much better view of how women should be. We don't have to have it all. We don't have to fix everyone and everything, and we must take care of ourselves.

The universe opened it up with such smoothness that it literally took my breath away. The house sold in five days, a replacement house found in one day. A 30-day escrow, and a "blip" on the credit bureaus, because someone in the mortgage company marked me down as dead. Through the emotional upheaval of having to go through the "widow" doldrums and trying to write without empathy, that my husband is dead, I looked at it as an exercise in humility. I smile, because it's all energy, and I will receive it as "all good."

Every morning, I visualize my practice of meditation in the Sierra foothills. The sound of laughter coming from granddaughters. The smell of the Thanksgiving turkey coming out of the oven in my new kitchen, with my family surrounding the table. Yes, that is good energy. That is positive energy, and THAT my friends, is inspired emotional manifestation!

Be grateful, and appreciate your abundance. These are the words you need to write down and post them on your refrigerator. Take the time to breathe, reflect, and feel your emotions. Life is so temporary, and if you want something to come to you easy, let it go and let it come. Be easy with yourself, and smile often. Laugh often. Laugh so hard that the tears run down your face! Love, that is all.

ABOUT THE AUTHOR: *LORI ANZINI*

When author Lori Godsey Anzini is asked to describe the beginning of widowhood, the spirited survivor answers with one word – grief. But Anzini doesn't stop there. She joyfully adds that sunshine does indeed come after the rain. In her first book, *Escaping the Jaws of Life: A Widow's Journey to Happiness* (published by AuthorHouse), she chronicles how she found joy after her husband succumbed to Parkinson's disease, and then brain cancer.

"Happiness comes in various forms," says Anzini, "but ultimately, I found that I was happiest when I purposely moved my intentions into pure positiveness, doing the things that I knew felt right. I became healthier, happier, and significantly drawn into my resolve that if I take care of myself first, then everything else is better."

In her intimate memoir, Anzini divulges the highs and the lows of caring for her husband during his illness and how she and her children dealt with the devastation of his death. Becoming a widow, admits Anzini, was a tumultuous journey. She credits the art of submission to helping her overcome her grief and flow, gracefully, into her next phase in life.

"When practicing the art of "letting go"my life dramatically changed towards a different path – one of spirituality, mystical belief, freedom, and acknowledging that my path unfolded the way it was supposed to go, and nothing is ever wrong," explains Anzini.

Anzini lives in Northern California and has picked up on the writing of memoirs. For over 30 years she collected the genealogical lines of her family. After finishing her "Escaping" book, she decided to honor the grandmothers in her family. She has published the lives of two of the grandmothers she has selected. The series "Through My Grandmothers' Eyes" is a compendium of six women in her lineage. You can find more information about her writing pursuits at: www.lorianzini.com.

Chapter 12

From Delicious Me to Delicious We

By Dannah Lewis

What do I know about receiving?

Warm sun, hot coffee, delicious bagel with cream cheese and lox...and having someone show up in my life who is consistently and constantly adoring every molecule of me into a puddle of gratitude and yum!

Fast forward a few hours and now I'm sitting in a coffee shop in Sausalito bemused by my new love and in slightly bewildered wonder and awe of what it took to have this show up in my life. At the core of it, and my most sacred and true knowing, is that it required a magnitude of receiving that until now I just didn't have the capacity for. And 45 years into this lifetime I know exactly what it took, every choice, every experience, every limiting point of view that was cleared and every possibility of future acknowledged and choosing towards to be in this space.

For me getting from a me to a we wasn't 'the thing' I was asking for... creating a delicious me and then generating, creating and receiving a delicious we... that was the big, juicy ask and receive. This is something I've always known was possible in a way that is so much greater than what most people in this reality choose. It took me years to put words to it and there still aren't words for all if it because it's about an energy and what two people can create together with that energy that is so much greater than what I believe can be created alone. The words? Warmth, confidence, kindness, caring, nurturing, sensualness, sexualness, ease, joy, adoration, admiration, allowance and appreciation, to name a few.

The truth is that having any kind of relationship wasn't easy for me. I generally ended up either heart-broken or pining for someone that wasn't choosing me. There was always a sense of frustration and lack. Even my eight-year marriage had a sense of frustration and lack. And I'm so grateful for it, for the marriage and every man I've dated since the divorce because every one of them gave me more of me, every one of them contributed to me shifting the frustration and lack to an ease and abundance within myself. It was during, and after, my marriage that I really started looking at and asking questions about what was going on and showing up and at the core was a lack of receiving.

There was a lack of receiving myself, all of me, and a frustration in others not receiving me, all of me that was running the undercurrents of my life. I started asking questions about how to change it and what it would take. That was seven years ago. If I knew the journey, if I knew the depth that was required for me to go to, if I knew the intensity of what would come up for me would I have still chosen to change it? I want to say I'm not sure when what I know about me is that I am tenaciously seeking consciousness and the joy of embodiment as a constant, aggressively present demand in this lifetime.

A quick rewind 45 years and you will find me starting this lifetime in a home of anger, rage, fury and hate. We come into this world beautiful beings of light and love and joy, open to gifts of the Universe and the gifts we have to contribute to the world by being…by simply being who we truly be. And for many, so many of us, that beauty and light and joy gets covered by this reality's version of other people's choices and limiting beliefs. How much of who you are today was created by thoughts, feelings and beliefs of your family you picked up before the age of two? Well, my before two and after two (until 11 when my parents divorced) was a home of domestic violence. Do I remember merry Christmases, fun summer vacations and warm, cozy nights at home? No, I don't.

I recall having to call 911 to have the police come to stop my father from beating my mother to death. I recall my mother leaving in the middle of the night to go to a shelter for safety. I recall always be on edge in a constant state of stress and always having the need to meet the requirements of a non-existent perfection impelled by my father in the insane hope of keeping the rage from imploding upon the household. That is the energy of my childhood. And I sincerely don't need to go into any more detail than that or to reason or justify anyone's behavior, actions or choices. It just was what it was. For a beautiful being of light and joy and love and openness to experience that well you start to shut down and do everything you can physically, emotionally, mentally and most profoundly, energetically, to control the energies you know, be, perceive and receive.

To clarify, for me, receiving is the capacity to be present with any and all energies without judgment. Simply being in allowance of everything that shows up and being in the question of what it is, what I can do with it, does it require to be changed, what contribution it can be to my life and to others. Cool?

Come forward again, not to today, to seven years ago when I started dating after my marriage ended. What a juicy learning experience that was! As I mentioned, the magical men in my life has been a blessing to me. I appreciate the women in my life, I have wonderful female friends, I know who has my back, I know who adores me, I know who I can play and create with and whom is in my inner circle of divas. Ahhh, but the men, the men have always dynamically contributed to the biggest changes I have been able to create for myself.

So I am so sweetly grateful for the magical men that have shown up in my life, particularly these past seven years to play with me.

There was the George Clooney look-a-like I dated right after landing in San Francisco that gave me the energies of excitement and enthusiasm for life. There was the dad of three that lived in the suburbs of Marin that gave me back my joy of sex and appreciation of music. There was the slightly brooding Pac Heights bohemian that gave me the gift of adventure and friendship. Oh my and the young one that gave me giggles and the pure innocent gift of moments of blissful yumminess. There are several more, each special to me for the experience we shared and the gifts of me they contributed to me discovering within myself. There was also a special contribution from a man I knew for over 20 years. We worked together, we played together and we shared a special connection that went beyond this reality. The day he died, I knew and it was one of my first recognizable experiences receiving the energy of entities (ghosts to some, beings without bodies to me).

This past summer when I was healing a broken heart, asking for what I actually require in romantic relationship, and making the demand for that greatness to show up, his energy was very present in my life. What was I still unwilling to receive about me that if I would receive it would generate and create the big, juicy 'yum' I was asking for? As I swam endlessly in my friend's warm, sunny pool surrounded by redwoods I would ask this question over and over again. And I kept hearing, 'you're beautiful, you are so f'ing beautiful and kind and caring and sweet and creative and have the capacity to see limitless dimensions of architecture of things and possibilities that exist for yourself and others with total ease and space and gratitude." And I didn't just hear this once, I heard it over and over again with such potency and clarity and admiration, acknowledgement and adoration it melted my molecules into puddles of gratitude.

What can gratitude do that nothing else on the planet can do? Annihilate judgment! Judgment cannot exist in the space of gratitude and having that much gratitude pushed my limits of receiving in a way that was 'preparing' me for something I knew was possible but hadn't experienced yet. What else 'prepared' me for great and continuously exponentializing receiving all these years? Discovering and choosing the transformational work of Access Consciousness®. For the past three years I have been taking classes, receiving the energy work, learning, facilitating private sessions and group classes with the tools that unlock trauma, drama, limiting beliefs from the body, brain and being. Where I'm going next would not have been possible and could not have shown up without adding this to my own processing, framework and intuitive powers for creating my life.

As I was launching my Delicious Dating class a few months ago, I myself was casually dating, building my business and generally enjoying life while wondering how to create even more deliciousness for myself. And then I saw it. While swiping through pictures on an online site app I saw a picture of a man that absolutely grabbed my attention. I remember thinking, 'I want to cuddle with that man' quickly followed by 'ummm, I wonder what it would take to meet him?' So I swiped right and he did too and we had a date arranged very quickly. The first date was fun and easy. During the texting while he was out of town before our second date I remember being very aware of the energy between us growing and shifting. Dates two to five occurred four nights in a row and we've been together as many nights since then as we possibly can (with schedules and kids permitting).

I was standing in my brother's kitchen chatting with my sister-n-law and she asked me, 'what is it about this guy?' I smiled, really widely and said, 'when I saw his picture I wanted to snuggle with him. He's so warm and kind and confident and sexy and nurturing and generous and talented. He is so expressive with his thoughts and affection. We play really well together and enjoy each other so much!" From the first date he has consistently and constantly expressed his joy, desire and excitement for me, us and what is possible for us to create together. And I am exactly the same with him and that, as I reminded myself this past summer, is a requirement I have for choosing to create a romantic relationship with someone. And that, as I realized this past summer required an amount of receiving I hadn't been to have… until now.

He acknowledges my beauty and kindness and caring and sweetness along with so many other things with such potency and clarity and admiration it melts away any residue of the stress of this reality. And just a few short months ago I recall the whispers of a similar acknowledgement pushing my edges of to an intensity I hadn't been able to receive... until now. He adores and appreciates every molecule of my body and being in a way that melts me back to the beautiful being of light and joy and love that I came into this world as... and wasn't able to return to... until now. When he places his hand(s) on me, it is the kindest most endearing, accepting and nurturing touch I have ever experienced and that melts away every judgment I've ever had of myself into a space of gratitude that I was so not willing to have and receive of this magnitude... until now.

Until now this magnitude of receiving was a theory. It was something I knew was possible but had not yet experienced. And I wonder where it will all lead. And I bet you're wondering if it will last. Well, there are no guarantees. Love and falling in love are not what create the big, juicy yum of a relationship outside of this reality. Love and falling in love are just the beginning. The inspired actions of loving, honoring each other, adoring each other, acknowledging each other, appreciating each other and choosing to nurture, care for, play with each other with joy and sensuality and sexualness that generates and creates the big, juicy yum. I know for sure that now I can receive it. Maybe not always gracefully, but I will absolutely choose to be in the question of what else is possible? And to be on the creative edge of 'Delicious We' in my constant demand for asking and receiving everything this universe can provide and over-deliver.

ABOUT THE AUTHOR: *DANNAH LEWIS*

Dannah Lewis, Founder of Delicious Life-Styled (www.DeliciousLifeStyled.com) and Certified Access Consciousness® Facilitator, is a lifestyle design and business consultant, taking people from possibilities to creating their juiciest realities with a deep sense of inspiration, caring, empowerment and celebration of living.

Her holistic approach merges 20+ years of corporate experience, creative talents and innate sense of working with energy and healing capacities to dynamically facilitate people and businesses to exceed their desired results. You will often hear her refer to this as "Framework & Flow".

Dannah lives in San Francisco, CA. She is a fanatic of fabulous food; seeker of joyful bliss; curator of delicious moments; creator of a juicy business; constant chooser of education and contributing to others; chaser of the sun and sultry swimming pools; lover of the city, mistress of nature giving North Bay / Marin and muse of the world.

Chapter 13

Embracing Your Story

By Patricia Dennis

Just lately, I asked my grandson what he wanted for his birthday and his reply warmed my heart. "Grandma… just give me one of those story photo books you do for us." How sweet was that! He acknowledged my passion for sharing life with pictures and words. I like to think of myself as a memory catcher using photography to assist in the art of storytelling. Since I was a youngster, my camera lens and writing have been the instruments I have used to celebrate the wonderful world we live in!

We all are born with talents. It is our choice whether to expound upon these or not. Sometimes life seems too complicated and we don't recognize how important it is to let our light shine! But then there comes that moment in time when we stop, take a deep breath, step forward and make our personal statement! My message is 'take' the time to acknowledge your gifts and don't be afraid of sharing them. It never is too late.

As I neared my 60th birthday, it was a time of retrospection and remembering the years that had passed. It was time to shake the composite corporate identity that I had for most of my life. I had worked for large companies, and bowed to their bid and call. The routine was the same, get up in the morning, work during the day, sleep at night, and play on the weekend. Sounds familiar doesn't it? After spending over 13 years of my life in this role, circumstances changed and I was unceremoniously discharged and thrown out into the world. Instead of being devastated I was actually elated and looked at it as a new beginning. With arms open wide I was ready and willing to receive the opportunities! This was also a time where I stopped and looked back over the years. How many times have we heard the phrase, "Have a plan B", when you retire? Well here I was partially retired and reaching for that plan B. I didn't have far to go and turned to what had fed my soul throughout the years. Photography and writing had always been my companions. Getting words down on paper was my way of clearing my head and my heart and then capturing those feelings with photographs put it all into perspective.

As a youngster, writing was an escape for me. I wasn't a very secure child but when I wrote I became invincible. My parents gave me many opportunities to succeed and I was blessed with being enrolled in every imaginable activity. You name it: Piano, ballet, gymnastics, drama and art, I was there. At six years old I was the youngest in an oil painting class and at age nine I was writing little stories that were published in the school paper. I felt quite important and took pride in the fact my parents were so aware of my many talents. So imagine how far I crashed when as a preteen I overheard my mother chatting to her sister, "We keep trying to get Patricia into activities to find something she is really good at. Jim bought her a camera and we're hoping that helps. We just don't know how to channel her imagination." What was this?! I wasn't the next ballroom genius or Picasso? There was one thing certain, imagination I did have. Writing and art provided the outlet and now here I was 12 years old and just handed my first Brownie camera! The world was indeed my canvas! I know my parents were thinking that this was a way to keep me amused. It worked! They probably had no idea that this one gift would open a door that would last a lifetime.

Now many years later here I was about to start another new chapter in my life. I no longer had to work a 9 to 5 job and my two young sons were now men with lives of their own. I had, as they say, 'paid my dues' and set my foundation. It was time to open the door to the possibilities. It didn't really take me long to embrace what I wanted to do. It is what I had always done. Here was the opportunity to bring my passion to the front line. The purpose was there but more important there was also the time available to relax and just be. There is so much beauty around waiting to be explored and my camera is one of the tools I use to capture those moments. For me, picking up a camera is much more than point and shoot. It is a communion between the lens, the soul and the subject. It is a matter of energy sharing. It virtually allows me to stop time and be open to receiving things I would have otherwise missed. The art of photography is also not just what I 'see' but what I can open up for others to see.

As much as it was important for me to embrace the artist within myself I knew that it was also important to be able to share these feelings and images. In the blink of an eye things can change so quickly and be lost. In the background there was that driving force to share my passion and also to leave a legacy. We all have been faced with losing loved ones and in our hearts regretted not having their stories captured so we could enjoy them again. Looking back at my parents lives I felt the loss of not being able to pick up a journal, or a documented photo book. I have memories, but will my children be able to share those memories of their grandparents? Will they be able to wiggle with delight about the story of Grandpa riding the pet cow to school, or feel the hunger in their bellies as Grandma talks about eating nothing but oatmeal for weeks? What pictures will they gather in their minds?

It really is an ironic twist of fate it is that it isn't until our later years in life when we have lost loved ones, and ourselves are facing our mortality that we desire to leave some sort of legacy. The years in between can be lost so quickly. My own mother made a feeble attempt to piece her life together during the last few months of her life. "What will you remember me by" she would cry. "Your father was so dynamic and everyone wanted to hear his stories. What were my stories compared to his?" Oh mom, you were so wrong! We would have welcomed being able to read about your early childhood and the ups and downs of your own life. When my mother died, my sister, brothers and I were left with picture albums that had no 'explanation' of who these people were in my parents' lives. We found poems that told of lonely times and loss during World War II. Did our mother write them? We'll never know. We do know they touched her heart and she kept them throughout the years. My mother was quiet, she was a private person and when she died, we were left to try and piece together the stories of who she really was. At this point I made a vow to seriously write down my stories as they happened and document them with photos. I did not want my own children to wonder about my life and I didn't want that for myself. Leaving a journal of the happenings in my life, could be the best keepsake I could leave my family. It would be something that could be looked at throughout the years.

We may not all be noted humanitarians, politicians, or celebrities, but each one of us is an individual and our lives are important! We should all be open to receiving and acknowledging our personal gifts. Stories should be documented! Time does put a different perspective on outcomes and there is so much to be learned when you take the time to go back and reminisce on your memories. It makes it more important being able to share these with your loved ones.

So yes, after leaving the 9 to 5 job I stepped into my own chapter and turned to what had been consistent in my life.

There was a fleeting feeling of regret, wishing that I had done this sooner. Now, however, it was the time to embrace who I was and what made me happy. I accepted that it was ok to spend hours writing or taking photos if that is what it took to get a finished product. And in some instances it was ok if nothing was completed. It was all part of the building blocks. Trial and error, passion, tears and joy all contributed to the creative juices. The pen went to the paper. Stories and poems were written for me and my family. Photos were paired with words and lovingly bound for the future stating this is who I am.

It was all made worthwhile that one day when my Grandson replied "just give me one those story photo books you do for us." My family may have the picture albums and they may or may not remember the people in them, but they will always be able to pick up a little book, read a small excerpt, look at the photos and say "Yep, this is my Grandma."

By embracing what makes me happy and sharing my creative spark, I have recaptured that same thrill I had when I was 12! The world is my canvas!

Remember, there is no story that has yet to be told, or song that has yet to be sung. It is the manner of the presentation and our own essence that makes each special!

The Road Ahead

Open your eyes and read
what is already written
in the language of your heart
Those words may be the ones
that lead you straight ahead
It matters not whether there is a road to travel,
a bridge to cross,
or a mountain to climb
The difficulty of the journey is only in your mind.

Enjoy each moment!

ABOUT THE AUTHOR: *PATRICIA DENNIS*

Born and raised in California, Patricia Dennis resides in Campbell. Photography has always played a big part in her life. Since her early childhood she has always had a camera of some sorts in her hands. Traveling on family vacations with a brownie camera in tow, she got an early appreciation of the many wonders of the National Parks and wildlife.

Through life's journey, raising a family, work and hobbies, Patricia has always come back to art and photography as means of expression. "Photography makes me slow down. It has taught me the difference between looking and taking the time to really see and appreciate the visual poetry that exists around us. Going out on a photo shoot in the morning, and being able to experience the energy of our natural surroundings makes my day. Color, form, and light intrigue me and I find that when I see the world through the lens of a camera, time seems to slow down. Nothing can be taken for granted for there are always hidden treasures to be found."

Patricia currently participates as a volunteer on the Art Committee at Filoli in Woodside, CA and is a member of the Penn Women, Fine Art of America, GF club, and was a member of the Gallery of Saratoga. Her photographs have been shown in juried shows throughout the San Francisco Bay Area. She is also the author of the "Forest Princess" a small book about transformation, and several photo books.

For more information see Patricia's website http://www.pdennisphoto.com.

Chapter 14

Let Love Fill Your Body

By Guillaume Corbin

Life taught me that love is the most important aspect in our existence. Science today reveals that consciousness affects biology. A high quality of presence, an open heart and clarity of vision connects the innate intelligence to a powerful field of infinite possibilities. Knowing this, the main goal of every human being would be to unleash his or her resistance to allow his or her consciousness and his or her heart to emerge fully.

Early in life, I was fascinated by the suffering imprisoned within the body of people around me. I asked myself questions like: Why would someone be so rigid, sad and live without passion? Why would someone accept to live a life that is not aligned with his deep essence? Why would an individual accept to lower his or her quality of life? What would be the cost for this individual and humanity? Are there tools, techniques, ways, and guides that exist that could assist those people, also a huge part of humanity? If so, why don't they use it? Am I part of it? Do I have any resistance in my body or my nervous system that keeps me from being who I really am? If so, should I do something about it? And what?

Later in life, I realized that I unconsciously adapted to society, moving far further away from who I really was as many of us do. Doing so enabled me to fit in with my friends and surroundings, making it easier to succeed in society. In time, I paid the a high price; I developed a stiff body, had a small understanding of me, had some difficulty relating with others, and was filled with fears and doubts which were holding me back from expressing who I really am in this world. I've always seen somehow the harmony and the potential in me and others, but I couldn't find the way to live otherwise.

Fortunately, I found mentors like Arno Burnier D.C., Pierre Bernier D.C., Christine Bourque D.C. and Donald Epstein D.C., who guided me to release pain in my body, deepen my connection to my inner heart, and reconnect to my essence. Everything changed when chiropractic entered my life. I am filled with immense gratitude to live this chiropractic philosophy since 1997, whose purpose is to reconnect and reunite the body and its innate intelligence to the universal intelligence. The result is a greater life expression on all levels of our existence. We experience life more fully, allowing our consciousness to expand and letting our innate potential express totally who we are in this world.

Now, according to my experience, living healthier means embracing the high energy of love vibrating within the body. We show up to what ignites us. We live in a free body and an open spine. We create life in an inspired way. We are connected to self, others and life while experiencing healthy, and rewarding relationships. We know who we are and we express it in our actions and words. By our very presence, we increase the energy level of others.

We have ALL the resources, love, and energy inside of us to live a thriving life. To get there, being opened and exposed is key. Say yes; surrender to oneself and to the flow of energy within our body and life without blocking it when judgment takes the lead.

It is said in biology that a living organism is naturally expressing more actions - which means that its energy is invested in creating more energy and reorganizes at higher levels of complexity ever seeking evolution and thriving. It facilitates change helping a person to use its free energy to do more. When used appropriately, both the free energy increases and the ability to work also, enabling us to accomplish bigger goals, serve more people, earn more money or whatever the outcome is that you are trying to achieve.

Conversely, when we are trying to create change by using inauthentic strategies that are incongruent with our nature, we exhaust our free energy accomplishing less. We are putting energy into a system of change that cannot generate an energy rich outcome. We are literally throwing good energy away.

From Resistance to Expansion

I work with three steps to allow the energy of receiving to flow through the body and life. These steps enrich the quality of health in general, our relationship with ourselves and others, our relationship with abundance and connection with our essence and our heart.

1. Embrace and unleash your resistance

2. Create and allow movement

3. Access your greatness and your heart

We are dynamic beings. As we integrate a step, we revisit it later in life with a deeper knowing and a new perspective, so we grow.

Embrace and Unleash your Resistance

Resistance can take form in the body as: tension, pain, diminished range of motion, armor, and protection, including living in fear, doubt, duality, and creating a low quality of living. When we're stressed out, anxious, overwhelmed, fearful, in pain and nothing seems to work, it's time to discover something new. Instead of trying to fight or flee the symptoms, it's time to reconnect to your suffering and injuries and begin to seek the attention your body needs.

To experience this healing and beyond, I recommend tools that assist in:

- Experimenting a deep connection to our mechanism of protection.

- Releasing large amounts of tension and energy stored in our tissues.

- Breathing more fully.

- Developing more discernment of what the body needs.

- Improving the posture and flexibility.

- Discovering the relationship between stress and its symptoms.

- Enhancing the ability to handle life stress and challenges.

Here are the kinds of questions you'll ask when you live mostly in resistance: Why me? Why not me? Why does this happen to me? Who was wrong/right? Why am I stuck? Why am I so blocked? Why do I keep doing this?

We are blocked because we perceive ourselves as not being good enough, so we adapt and change to fit the needs of others. This makes us feel like a victim, far from our power.

We feel like we have what we don't want or we're not having what we want!

We don't find the way out because this acts as a blind spot in our body, and we tend to deny our unconscious conditioning. When we dissociate from a part of ourselves that we cannot accept, we turn off the energy in that part of the body. It's the ego mechanism to fight, flight or freeze to protect our stories.

In a duality state of consciousness, we judge things as right or wrong, good or bad. We seek for the savior and we tend to find a guilty party. In duality, our body is stiff and disconnected in certain parts while others are connected, stronger and free. When we stop being ourselves, we take on behaviors that limit our ability to see the endless possibilities in every situation. We are stuck in a pattern and remain frustrated. Our perception of the world is distorted and our ability to respond appropriately is compromised.

Our stories may have served us until now but we can decide otherwise. All we need is engagement, courage, and willingness to go through the journey. No excuses, no justifications. The pain is not *out there* but *in here*. The pain is not to be avoided but is a motivator, a fuel for change. Marie-Von Ebner-Eschenbach said that "pain is the great teacher of mankind. Beneath its breath, souls develop". It actually takes a huge amount of energy to hold resistance and stories. Releasing them enhances the energy of receiving.

It's important to practice self-observation with no identification or trying to fix anything because you're not broken. Simply be aware, acknowledge and accept what comes up and most importantly, breathe it in!

Create and Allow Movement

To allow fully the movement in our body and our life we must crave for it. It's a choice.

When we play small to avoid discomfort that moment is our opportunity to reclaim our power. Do you want to challenge yourself? Yes! So learn to stop withholding mental conditioning, take control of your destiny and claim your energy to live fully, to create something new for you.

To experience this healing and beyond, I recommend tools that assist in:

• Increasing the level of energy and courage to take back fully our power of creation.

• Stopping in a genuine and profound way holding on to what no longer serves us.

• Expressing who we are.

• Changing our stress into fuel for our growth and development.

• Developing our strength, focus, capacity of decision, direction and clarity.

• Changing to a lifestyle that promotes a high level of energy.

• Exiting the need to react in life with stress, defense and tension.

Here are the kinds of questions we'll ask when we are ready to move forward: What can I do to never disempower myself again? How can I express my courage? How can I face this now? What can I do to really be ready? How can I conduct an inventory and get rid of what no longer serves me?

At a certain moment, we experience confusion when we decide to go past the point where we usually shut down, because we finally take the leap that we could never make by ourselves. We don't understand life on the other side of the fear that keeps us small. All our emotions tell us to stop. Our mind says it's a bad thing but some part of us, says it's okay. By this time we have healed enough to listen to it and invite it back to us. And we jump into the swirling confusion. And then life is never the same. We grow. We don't know how or why but it is okay and we trust even though we are scared. Suddenly everything becomes fluid and a new vibration takes over.

The mental wants to control everything; if we stay there we won't be able to connect fully to the spiritual aspect of our being. Merging all sensations to the heart to what comes up in our body and life without any resistance is important, otherwise, we go back. To surrender authentically to the body is to create the experience in here instead of out there.

It is in our presence within this new space, in the emptiness that we can receive completely. It's now time to create a movement, a breathing and a particular energy to allow and access the spiritual aspect of our being. God is not out there anymore but within us.

Access your Greatness and your Heart

When we grow beyond the conditioning, the world awaits us. Why are we here? Who are we really? How I could participate in the circle of life? As your waking consciousness well beyond what we think possible and what life should be, we become what we want to see in this world and we discover our place in this world.

To experience this healing and beyond, I recommend tools that assist in:

- Connecting to the presence of energy beyond the matter.

- Growing compassion, forgiveness, gratitude, and joy even in life's challenges.

- Hosting a rich life in the vibration of the heart.

- Deepening an awareness of our essence.

- Being aware in our body of the spiritual experience in the present moment.

- Noticing the phenomenal increase of our ability to adapt and our ability to contribute to a better world for us and humanity.

• Developing the spirit of community in which our only presence and others influenced the world in which we live. Our lives are gifts for everyone, we just need to give and receive in love.

Here are the kinds of questions we'll ask when we want to express our greatness: How can I express more love, more gratitude? What gift has been given to me? How do I give my gifts in joy and gratitude? Where is the gift in this? How can I receive others/circumstances with gratitude as gifts? Here are some questions to guide you:

1. If we were all-knowing and had the answer to everything, what would you tell yourself to do about the things that hold you back from being great?

2. How have the actions of others been the cause of many blessings in your life?

3. What is the biggest blessing that you bring to the lives of others?

When we connect to the consciousness of the energy of the Universe, we have access to the knowledge of everything because we are one with everything. With the knowledge that there is only love in the world, there is nothing to do but give love to others and receive it back. No duality anymore, such as good/bad, but we give and receive love as a gift. My presence is a necessary ingredient for the All. If someone hurts me, I'm not stuck with it like in the lower state of consciousness because I see love in everything. The suffering simply hides our gifts. Our being is a gift that makes the world what it is. Our lives are gifts to one another, whether we consciously receive them or not.

In true spiritual surrender the needs of the self as an individual become integrated with the needs of the whole. Our individual existence is inextricably linked with the universal community.

This too is an expression of wellness but with a wider definition than health in an individual human body. When this surrender is reached we don't need to have "the good thing" happen so long as what does happen is congruent with the highest good.

Conclusion: A Rich Life

A rich life passes through the body intelligence. Resistance, pain and tension are only a lack of love in a certain part of our body. The presence of the energy/vibration of love heals. Exponential growth happens when we highlight the aspects of our life that we allowed to be hidden, so far. Our greatness is related to the degree of love we welcome in our life and our body. So, we go increasingly from resistance, tension, protection to freedom, expansion, and love.

We could spend our life in breakthroughs but we're already where we want to be. Go get the energy in our internal resistance, courage and from all the external source of power available in order to live a life in its fullest expression. Grow to live consciously physically, emotionally, mentally, and spiritually. So we create, we expose, we give to the world, and we receive.

As Rumi said, "Your task is not to seek for love but merely to seek and find all the barriers within yourself that you have built against it". Happiness is in us, in our spiritual and heart connection. Just let it shine!

ABOUT THE AUTHOR: *GUILLAUME CORBIN*

Guillaume Corbin is a doctor of chiropractic. He shares his gifts with passion and love by showing up for himself and to the world. He plays full out to guide people to reach a higher state of consciousness in the full expression of the human potential in a high quality of presence.

In 2005, he was introduced to Epstein Technologies which includes Network Spinal Analysis™ (NSA) and Somato-Respiratory Integration™ (SRI).

NSA is a chiropractic approach developed by Dr Donald Epstein D.C. that cues the body and its innate intelligence to reconnect, release and transform its physical, emotional and mental resistances to ease the access to our heart, to our inner wisdom and to our greatness.

SRI are exercises based on Donald Epstein's book *The 12 Stages of Healing*. It is designed to offer new options in the experience of the body and the personal healing. It educates to listen to the body's rhythms and inner wisdom through focused attention, gentle breath, movement and touch.

The care with Guillaume goes far beyond the sessions on the chiropractic table. With lectures, individual and group sessions, he seeks to educate and inspire to assist you to achieve new levels of wellness.

He allows your expansion and integration of unresolved. He guides you to what requires your attention and to discern what goes up and assists you through the choices available to you in order to have the greatest impact on your body, your life and your community.

He inspires to accept and receive the wonderful gifts giving to us and to give wholeheartedly who we are to the world.

He works with 3 steps to go from resistance to expansion in order to allow the energy of receiving to flow through the body and life.

1. Embrace and unleash your resistance
2. Create and allow movement
3. Access your greatness and your heart

These three steps enrich the quality of health in general, our relationship with ourselves and others, our relationship with abundance and connection with our essence and our heart.

He is co-author of two books, *Devenir soi* (2011) and *Dire oui à la Vie!* (2013) published by Dauphin Blanc. He is a TV columnist at Cogeco television for the Oui à la vie! show since 2012. He did 2 missions in Guatemala and Bolivia with Chiropractors Without Borders.

He practices with his wife Cloe Lapointe D.C., in St-Sauveur, Québec, Canada.

Find out more on Guillaume's work or contact him at: www.strategiesante.ca.

Chapter 15

Be Open to Receive

By Sheila Murrey

In order to receive what you want - you need to be open. Your wants and desires may be many, wonderful health, wealth, or wisdom - all manner of blessings but for these things to come - you must **be open** to receive.

Expanding your awareness of different perspectives brings new possibilities. When you let go of your need to be right, which comes from the ego, new experiences are birthed. When you let go of the need to interpret the world according to your beliefs (programming) - the possibilities are endless as to what you can receive.

For your consideration, I share some fresh thoughts to help you open to more:

- Do whatever you have to do to stay **awake** and **aware** of what's happening around you - even if it means you have to put a pebble in your shoe

• Learning should be lifelong because change is inevitable

• Go with the **flow**, be as water (flow over and around obstacles)

• Understand that you'll learn your **whole life** - you don't have to know it all today

• Make every effort to **enjoy (In Joy)** where you are

• It is **not** your responsibility to be **perfect** - just show up

• There is a perfection in the imperfection

• You do not need to **solve** every problem in the world

• You probably do **not really** know it all

• Take whatever you can **use** from what's being said, let the rest go

• Pay most attention to what **aligns** with your soul

• **Really** pay attention if it keeps coming around

• Observe your **thoughts** - gently nudge them into alignment with your soul

• Let the inappreciable **things** take care of themselves

• One day you may come to know that everything has value

- It is possible to appreciate it all

- **Don't judge** - leave alone (or behind) whatever doesn't serve you. *Nobody likes a whiner, complainer, name caller, or nag (all judgments).*

- Learn and share - continue to learn your lessons even as you give to others

- As much as you can, be grateful for everything (even when you think you can't)

There's a familiar story many have written or spoke of that speaks of a man who waited on God to save him during a storm or flood. While the man fervently prayed for God to save him from the raging or rising water, someone offered him a ride in a truck, but the praying man said **"no thanks, God will save me"**... awhile later a boat called out to him, but he declined their offer of help too. Eventually a helicopter arrived offering rescue but a third time, the man yelled, "no thanks, God will save me". After the man drowned he asked God why he hadn't saved him. God said, "Well I sent you a truck... then I directed a boat your way... and later even a helicopter..." the point of the story is **the man was so convinced** he knew **how** God would save him (no doubt in some miraculous way so he could brag about it) that when the other normal natural offers of help came, the man **wasn't paying attention, nor** was he **open** to **receive**.

Every time I hear that story it reminds me about people

praying for relief from their pain / illness / suffering (okay maybe they aren't praying to God, they are going to doctors) and God sends them help via their friends, coworkers, new and interesting books, natural remedies, better food, nutritional therapies, divine / energy healing, shaman or other and **they scoff**... they would rather **SUFFER** and die with that illness before opening to receive any natural help God is providing. How sad!

I often meditate on that story and ask myself what am I blocking out or "**saying no to**" that perhaps God is sending me for my highest and best? Instead, I don't consider it; much less allow because somehow I think **I know better**? I am quite sure this is one reason my mother initially attempted to discourage me from going to college. She thought the more educated people became the more they would lean to their own understanding and the less they'd listen to the **still small voice of God**.

I don't necessarily think educated people ignore God, as I know many scholarly folk who daily meditate to receive divine direction. I think experience sometimes causes us to think, I've already experienced this and learned my lesson - so why do it again?

- I've been **married** twice before so why marry a third time? *Uh, because I'm blissfully happy this time around and I could have missed out on a wonder-filled marriage!*

- I've lived other **places**, why move again? *Because I love* *variety, challenge, and all new kinds of experiences.*

• I've already changed **jobs** umpteen times, why change again? *Because this job really aligns with my soul and I get paid the most I've made in my career!*

• I've already tried this or that **diet**, why try another? *Because though I am gloriously healthy, I used to weigh less and I miss that body shape.*

• I've already bought **supplements** and still have capsules in my cabinet I haven't taken, why buy yet another brand? *Because perhaps the next formulation will actually resolve whatever the issue is.*

Oddly enough, I used to make a joke and tell coworkers and friends, "I'm not happy unless I am complaining about something"! Yes, I used to say that – me the self-help author! Haha! Wow have I changed! I am so thankful to all of my mentors and teachers (I've thanked many of them publicly in my blog)!

All I am suggesting to you, my dear sweet reader, is to **consider being open** to receive new insights, especially if the help that is coming your way **won't hurt you**, has **no side effects**, takes **very little effort** on your part, or allows you to make **small changes** over time. Yes believe me, even you're taste buds can change. You do **not** need sugar. There is no such thing as a sugar, caffeine, grain, dairy, alcohol, or soda-pop **deficiency**. Oh, I forgot those were notes to myself about dietary choices, not yours (but feel free to take my advice about that too, if you like – smile).

Story 1 - Coffee

Until recently I've not been a coffee drinker (love the aroma but dislike the flavor) but after my husband and I watched a documentary, "Healing Matrix: The Hidden Power of Coffee" with Dave Asprey on Gaiam TV (via our Spiritual Cinema Circle monthly DVD subscription) my husband decided to try adding butter and coconut oil to his morning coffee! After he tried it for a few weeks I decided to try it (blending mine in a blender like Dave Asprey and Regina Meredith did) and I've begun losing weight and have realized I also have more energy - even using decaf!

What did I receive?

- Something new in common with my husband
- More energy
- Another weight loss aid
- Improved cognitive brain function

Some say not to have an open mind because our brains may fall out, but I think that's goofy! Our brains aren't literally going to fall out, nor do I think we'll be gullible to "fall for anything" – at least not for very long. I think that's a lie from the deceiver. This is the same deceiver who enjoys dividing people in order to conquer.

I believe it's a better world when we can focus on bringing people together. I am all about inclusion not exclusion. Don't like someone? That only hurts **YOU** in the long run. That person you don't like doesn't care (and probably doesn't even know you don't like them!) but the cells of **your** body are listening to your thoughts! You not liking someone can cause your cells to vibrate in a way that begins to set up dis-ease in your body!

Perhaps it's just human nature though to disagree rather than look for our commonalities?

Story 2 - Good vibrations

One day I found it amusing that a woman whom I usually experienced weird vibes around announced within earshot of me that she "**loves all people!**" I was shocked! She seemed so heady and introverted. Had I misjudged her?

I decided to allow myself the space to open to new insights. Weeks later this same gal shocked me again when she declared that **she got more work** done in another setting and when less work got done "that's what they got" for moving her! Immediately I put my judge hat on and thought to myself it sure seemed she was making a perfect excuse to be late on future work!

I knew I did not like how this situation made me feel though so, I began to pray about my conundrum before going into my stair-climbing meditation.

What did I receive?

- Commonalities are more important to me than any differences

- I learned I still judge - even though I thought I'd quit judging others

- I realized the importance of "clearing statements"

I learned this woman had long held some strong opinions on past historical events. Undoubtedly that's what I had been sensing to feel those "off" vibes. I knew I had to do some clearing work around these feelings. I began to gently question her "limiting beliefs" determined to only remain open to conversing so, if nothing else, I could learn anything I was supposed to learn from this child of God.

Happily, though not always easily, I found we shared many commonalities:

- God, power of prayer, and Christianity

- Love for God and people

- Love of all things holistic

- Vast natural health remedy know-how
- Logic and intelligence
- Belief in teamwork and sharing
- Extensive knowledge about organic whole foods
- Inspired others to eat better
- Multi-lingual
- Plethora of cultural experiences

No way was I going to shut myself off from this astute gal just because she had a couple of beliefs that differed from mine. So, anytime I began to judge I would gently guide my thoughts along these lines:

- Beliefs are where it's at, all day, every day, and everywhere
- Love God, allow and love all living things
- As I believe, God saves me
- As I open, God directs me
- The only separation is when I pull away, or resist.
- As I believe, I receive

- As I give, I receive - it ALL flows through me

- Life really is always GOOD!

The best part was that this woman motivated me to begin a daily stair-climbing habit that I continue to this day!

Story 3 – I know a Secret

A new acquaintance shared that he did not believe in "**The Secret,**" or Law of Attraction (LoA).

Admittedly when "The Secret" first came out I wanted nothing to do with it. I had my own Christian belief system at that time and did not feel I needed to delve into whatever it was. However, I have since become very adept at being able to explain LoA in fairly simple terms – to sort of demystify it.

I simply told this gentleman that LoA is like gravity, it exists whether you want to believe it or not and that also like gravity you can't see it, but you sure can see the Universal organizing effects of it!

When you **feel excited** about something you are more apt to talk about it, laugh, smile, and express **JOY**. When you're happy, enjoying life, all kinds of doors open to you! What's the **benefit** of being happy? Being happy!

Conversely, when you feel bad nothing works. You labor to get out of bed. You stub your toe on a table that has never moved and you've known for years where it is. You lose your car keys, glasses, or phone. Walk around with a big old frown on your face and you know it drives people away from you. You're fighting with yourself about something. Let go of whatever you're resisting and your day will improve.

What was received?

- Happiness quotient has increased for both of us

- I discovered how much in common I have with a Marine

- I am a living example of a subject I knew nothing about ten years ago

- Every day is a gift!

Story 4 – Maybe the Eyes Really do "have it"!

A friend described a time when she was providing chair massages and a man she'd never met kept staring at her. She is intuitive (as I believe many of us are) and could almost physically feel his gaze upon her backside. When she had finished with one client she asked this man (who I'll call the "watcher") if he wanted to go next. He simply replied, "I'm OK".

Reading my friend's story the first time I didn't quite understand why she had the reaction she had. She described it well, but somehow (for me) I knew I had missed something important about it. Perhaps just my reading words to retell of the encounter it did not include the **fullness** of it? After meditating on this for a couple days (because I am a student of **all things energy**) I realized that when I read her words they could not include **ALL** of the vibration, which had occurred at the time of the exchange of information between my friend and the watcher.

From the lens of my experience it didn't seem that the watcher's brief response was inappropriate. Yet in the moment, my friend interpreted his words quite differently, allowing what he said to "ruffle her feathers" so to speak. Perhaps his words were incongruent with the vibes he was putting out. Could it be that the watcher had unwittingly provided my pal with unseen **vibrational** information?

We may not always be able to explain why someone makes us feel the way we feel, especially if they give us the creeps, but that feeling can often seem just as real as if we'd been physically touched. Why?

In elementary school I learned that all objects are made of fast moving molecules. That means there is energy and space between molecules. But, what makes up our thoughts? Certainly thoughts are not solid. Yet most of us put a lot of stock in our judgments and even place a considerable importance on our **interpretations!** We all know people can get pretty touchy about some of their opinions – especially when their perceptions are based upon limiting beliefs!

In an episode of Divine Cosmos, David Wilcock shared Dr. Ignacio Ochoa Pacheco's, scientific research (from the paper titled: Ultrastructural and light microscopy analysis of SAPA bions formation and growth in vitro, from the orgone.org website). David provides photos on an exciting experiment on his DivineCosmos.com website where they took sterilized sand (I am paraphrasing) and let it sit 24 hours undisturbed in a **sealed test tube** and watched as hidden, unacknowledged 'torsion fields' gathered up the raw materials in the tubes and start creating DNA - and life! Communication was going on within the sealed test tube!

What was received?

- Science proves something unseen communicates
- We are always receiving—some way, some how
- Perhaps the eyes really are the "windows of the soul"
- Be unbounded and full of possibilities to see how it all becomes what it is
- Stop trying to defend your perceptions and open to consider new ways
- It's really cool when old things become new again

In the womb I was made from everything my mom breathed, ate, drank, thought, and felt so that I would be able to handle whatever was in her environment. I had no say about those things. However, as an adult if I want to make a change to better myself in some way the way it seems to work is:

- If you want to be great, surround yourself with all that is great

- If you want to be a teacher, appreciate and hang out with teachers

- If you want to be a singer, allow great singers to mentor you and surround yourself with all things musical

- If you want to speak another language fluently with perfect native-like pronunciation, immerse yourself with that language, talk with people who speak it, watch TV and movies in that language and so forth

I have **become** from **what is all around me** and what is around me is in different phases of existence.

Humans tend to think a lot about **competition** and **conquest** but I feel all that need to conquer stems from our desire to fight or hold resistance to what is.

I have learned that it's sure easier to go with the flow, join, agree, and just be. We're all here to **quest**, just don't con-quest. Pick a leaf and eat, it is okay! You don't have to fight an animal to the death in order to eat. We really must love the **dramatic** because it seems we create a lot of drama in our lives when it's just not that necessary at all.

May you always be open to receive what's available for your highest and best and may peace be yours—and so it is.

ABOUT THE AUTHOR: *SHEILA MURREY*

Excited by life's possibilities, Sheila Murrey has already achieved so much in life: maintaining a loving relationship with gifted songwriter guitarist husband Richard, the nearly single-handed raising of two children whom are now thriving adults, and totally enjoying the times she can visit with her three-year old granddaughter and celebrate her as the flutter of pure powerful source energy that she is!

Sheila is a software professional with an expansive, evolving career and engaging presence! She's passionate about natural and holistic wellness after finding a variety of natural herbal and food remedies plus holistic health treatments that freed her body of the asthma she experienced for nearly 30 years. Sheila QUIT five (5) pharmaceutical medications and no longer depends upon the allopathic health industry to feel good. Sheila took it upon herself to heal her body and knows others can too! Sheila uses her power as an author and speaker to promote her wellness passions (which, includes holistic and alternative health modalities, raw foods, energy medicine, and EFT / Tapping).

In the technical arena, Sheila is approachable and often is easily able to engage others about wellness topics while providing technical savvy. Sheila learned long ago it's difficult to work on long and arduous software projects when you're unhealthy or have aches and pains. She often refers others to quick remedies that provide relief and ease! Sheila desires to partner with sustainable conscious wellness or food companies and devotes a large part of her time to promoting natural and holistic health businesses via her articles on Examiner.com, working events and expos on the weekends, and crafting promotional videos. Sheila also sings duets with her guitarist husband - their original music rocks! You can often find them performing at local Florida "open mic" and private events.

Sheila's technical degrees are in business, communications, and digital design. Her vast and significant computing career spans twenty-five plus years and many roles, including: computer-aided business administration, software training, writing, testing, and analysis.

Her mission? To encourage others to live with integrity in spirit, mind, and body by always seeking to provide others with the most conscious natural and holistic wellness information and products. We Are All Connected. Think HAPPY!

You can check out all of the holistic health and natural beauty articles Sheila has written for Examiner at http://www.examiner.com/health-and-beauty-4-in-orlando/sheila-murrey

Sheila also invites you to get to know her more personally at: http://takeituponyourself.wordpress.com

Reach out to her at: sheila.murrey@gmail.com

Chapter 16

Live and Receive Pleased

By Kaarin Alisa

Here is the good news! The joyous and unequivocal truth is that receiving is your birthright. The first thing that happened to you when you were born was that you received: food, shelter, and hopefully love.

And as you grew you learned how to accept these gifts naturally every day. For the health of your body you received food and drink. For your mental health, you received love and support from your nearest and dearest. And for your spiritual health you received inspiration and peace from your communion with nature and your Source. If you didn't receive all of the above-mentioned gifts, you could not thrive.

At first, these may have been given to you without you asking for them, but at some point, you had to start requesting the things you needed and desired. To accomplish this, you were probably taught the same thing I was taught, to be polite when asking. You learned the common polite phrases "please" and "thank you". These words show respect to other people and to ourselves. Also, recognize that they are designed to ease our way through the process of receiving.

We say please when we want to politely ask for something, and we say thank you when the request has been fulfilled. Too often, however, the meaning of these words changed for us in response to our own ability, or lack thereof, to receive abundantly. When we feel undeserving of the gifts offered, or when we feel we don't deserve to ask for what we want, please can seem more like begging and thank you can seem like supplication.

Let's take back these phrases and realign them to their original meanings once more. Let's recover the joy of receiving and the knowledge that we deserve all that we desire. Let's start with a six-step solution that restores receiving to the position it should assume as a natural process where we are not begging or supplicating ourselves. Rather, we are reestablishing the very respect and joy that receiving has always meant to engender.

This process is simply called 'Please' and it incorporates the following steps:

1. Picture What You Want

2. Light Up Your Desire

3. Engage with the Unknown

4. Accept the Gift with Appreciation

5. Sense How the Gift Makes You Whole

6. Enjoy the Gift with Every Cell of Your Being

Step #1 – Picture What You Want

Get really clear about what you want to receive. You can't ask for something you don't understand. And you can't understand something unless you can picture it, in exquisite detail.

For example, say you want a new pair of socks. You have to know what socks are and be able to see the effects of socks in your life. You know socks wrap your feet, they shelter your feet from the cold and the harsh rubbing of shoes against your skin. When you need socks, you need them. If you don't have them you ask for them, but consider this: When you go to the store and ask the clerk for a pair of socks, she may have 100 varieties from which to choose. If you give her no more information than that, you may receive a pair of socks in a color you don't like and a size that does not fit you. So you give her more detail and finally after enough detail has been imparted, she can fulfill your request with exactly the right pair of socks for you.

It is the same with all requests; you have to know in detail what you are requesting for your request to be filled properly. So, give your thoughts structure. Picture the effects of your request in your life and know, before the request is fulfilled, the attributes you need. Now realize that perhaps not every detail of your request will be fulfilled with absolute precision, however, when you do place your order complete with the necessary details, there is a much greater probability that the fulfillment of your request will meet your needs and desires on most counts.

I once placed an order with the universe for a new car. I knew what I wanted to feel like when I drove the car. I knew the perks I wanted the car to have such as a great sound system, a sunroof, comfortable seats, a sleek look, etc... And I pictured the car being ice blue like the last car I owned. When my request was fulfilled, the car had all the perks I pictured and more, fulfilling not just my immediate requests, but surpassing them in many ways. It was the perfect car, but it was not ice blue. And when I sat in the driver's seat and revved up the engine, the color did not matter to me. It felt like the perfect car and that was what mattered. As it turned out, that make and model of car did not come with a blue option. I could have had it painted, but the color was an extraneous request that mattered very little to me once my request was fulfilled. That car served me well for many years and the best part of the package was that it cost a full $5,000 less than I was willing to spend. The universe was able to fulfill my request and give me MORE than I asked for, but only because I had given my request the details up front.

Step #2 - Light Up Your Desire

Once you have a picture in your mind, complete with your desired details, it's time to light up that picture with your desire, with your passion. Nothing comes to the apathetic, so banish apathy and feel strongly about what you are requesting.

This is not yearning, wishing for something to happen. This is seeing the request already made manifest in your life and feeling how it feels to have it. You own the picture. You make it yours. You feed the picture with the passion of your desire and it lights up like a beacon. The more passion and desire you feed into your picture the more urgency you create for its fulfillment.

Think of it like this: Picture going to the door of a neighbor and apathetically asking that neighbor to help you plant some flowers in the strip of garden that borders your yards. So you say, "I wonder if you might plant flowers with me, I mean if you want to, I mean you don't have to, it doesn't matter that much, but hey, I'm asking." Do you suspect your neighbor is going to help? Probably not. But say you ask this way instead, "Hi, I've got a bunch of bulbs I'd like to plant in that strip of dirt between our properties. They'd really liven the place up and put a smile on both of our faces. How about coming out and helping me plant them? We can get it done quickly together and the outcome would be so sweet!" You put passion in your request and now, even if your neighbor says no, he or she might bring you a glass of lemonade to hydrate you while you are planting, an unexpected treat!

The creative power of the universe listens the same way your neighbor did and will fulfill your request or otherwise help you move in that direction, but only if you ask with passion and desire.

Step #3 – Engage with the Unknown

Once you know what you want to receive, and you've fed it your passion, open up to the unknown. This is a part of the process that many call the adventure. It is sticking your toes in the water of life and moving beyond the staid confines that have held you in one place. You must move into life, into the mystery of all that is, for the universe to bring the raw materials of fulfillment to you.

This is a natural process and you have to meet it with a natural flow.

Try new things, go to new places, meet new people, drive on new streets, watch new programs on TV. If you always call your mother on Sunday, call her on Thursday instead. If you always buy your coffee with steamed milk, try mocha instead. If you always meet with your staff on Monday morning at 9, move it Tuesday once and see what happens. Mix it up and engage with the unknown.

The reason you do things that same way repeatedly is that you know what the results will be. But if you want something new to happen, some new request to be fulfilled, you can't do the same thing over and over and expect the result to change. That is Albert Einstein's definition of insanity. It's also the universe's excuse to leave you alone and THAT is EXACTLY what you don't want if you are asking the universe to fulfill a new request. You have to meet the universe where its creative force resides, in the mystery, in the unknown.

Step #4 – Accept the Gift with Appreciation

Here is where thank you comes in. When the universe fulfills your request, have a sense of appreciation for it. Even if the request was only partially filled, you must still appreciate what you received. If you have been plagued with having your requests fulfilled partially and in ways that do not satisfy you, perhaps this is what you are missing.

Going back to the example of the car I requested, I could have seen the color of the car and felt no appreciation for the otherwise perfect and exceptional fulfillment of my request. I could have said, "But it's not ice blue. Sorry, it's not what I asked for." That would have a put a stopper on all the energy that brought this car in the first place. It would have immediately negated everything and I would have had to start over at square one to have a new choice brought my way.

But even if the color was so important to me that I couldn't see past it to accept the universe's gift, it would serve me to appreciate that which did fulfill my request. Even if I had to ultimately say no to the car, I would need to acknowledge and be appreciative of the parts of the car that WERE prefect; the parts of the request that the creative force got right.

Several years ago, a young woman I know made a request to receive a life partner. She had very specific requirements in her request of what had to be true of this man when he arrived. She then proceeded to date a string of men that did not meet her criteria fully, but each one met her request in part. I counseled her to be appreciative of the parts she liked and to also continue to hone her request as she learned more and more about what was actually important to her.

After a series of these short-lived dating companions, she unexpectedly met a man at a party who ended up fulfilling her request almost to perfection. Did he match her first request? No, but did he match the last request, the one honed through the give and take of appreciation? Yes, almost completely and she found that, just as I had with the color of the car, the parts of her request that were not fulfilled were of little importance compared to the parts that were fulfilled.

The give and take of appreciation is how you provide feedback to the creative source that it can hear and work with. It opens the door to flow, rather than shutting the door and cutting off the flow.

Step #5 – Sense How the Gift Makes You Whole

Once you do receive an answer to your request, notice how it makes you feel whole. Don't hold the gift at arm's length.

Don't accept the gift, say thank you, and then put it on the shelf. Nothing clogs up your life more than stuffing gifts in the closet. This step doesn't just follow appreciation; it's the next level of appreciation. You bring the gift into your life and see how it fits. If you ask for a new food processor and you receive one for your birthday, it isn't the act of receiving that was the goal. The goal is to then take that food processor and incorporate it into your life. Set it up in your kitchen and make food with it!

This goes for all things you receive. Let the gifts become part of you, part of your life and see how they make you more whole. If they don't make you more whole, then pass them on, give them to someone who will make use of them and revise your request of the universe.

This advice isn't just for the things you clearly ask for. If you receive gifts you didn't ask for, do the same; show appreciation and sense how the gift makes you whole. Often we get a gift and think there is something wrong because we didn't get something that was on our manifestation list. Perhaps you asked for more clients in your business and what you got was a blue tie from Uncle Bob. But you didn't need a blue tie, in fact you already have several blue ties. Do you throw it in the garbage, rage at the universe that it wasn't what you asked for, and denigrate Uncle Bob in your mind for not giving you what you wanted? (Be truthful, I know I've done that in the past.) Do you think that after that recalcitrant display the creative source of the universe is going to keep bringing you gifts?

When you receive a gift you didn't ask for and it isn't what you wanted, find the gift in the gift. Find the characteristic or quality of the gift that DOES make you more whole. In the blue tie example, perhaps Uncle Bob gave you the gift with arm loads of love that came straight from his heart. In denigrating one part of the gift, you miss the part that was important, the part that when accepted, makes you more whole.

At the very least, every time you receive a gift, asked for or not, you can be assured you are currently open to receiving and that is the most salient point. Be thankful for that!

Step #6 – Enjoy the Gift with Every Cell of Your Being

What's left? Being with what you have received! Bringing it into your life, seeing it make you whole in whichever way it does and then enjoying it with every cell of your being. Going back to the car example, the last step for me was to use the car, enjoy driving in it, listen to the awesome sound system, roll back the sunroof, and feel the sun on my skin. Feel the same, or more, passion or joy at having received, than the passion of desire you put into your initial request.

This shows you are pleased. You asked to be pleased and you are. Don't hide this pleasure under a barrel and expect it to come out another day. The pleasure at having and using the things you requested is integral to the process and must be expressed.

The Time is Now

There are plenty of things to receive, throughout our life, that are not so pleasurable. The passion that some gifts will stimulate is not pleasure, but pain, grief, or confusion. But consider that when you are in a habit of not hiding your gifts in a closet, not sidestepping them with apathy, or holding them separate from yourself, you will stay in the flow of life. While in the flow helpers will come forward, opportunities will emerge, and gifts will continue to appear that will aid you in moving through the difficulties with grace.

It's the give and take of receiving that will always serve you. And remember, receiving is a natural part of life; it is your birthright. I wish for you many gifts, more wholeness, and plenty of exactly what you desire. I wish for you to live and receive pleased.

ABOUT THE AUTHOR: *KAARIN ALISA*

Kaarin Alisa CHT, is a catalyst for movement and transformation. She has honed her abilities as a change agent in the metaphysical and energetic arts for more than 40 years practicing as a spiritual adviser, clinical hypnotherapist, teacher, author, medical intuitive, and energy practitioner. She has helped scores of people realign to their highest truth, so they are then free to pursue their dreams and ambitions.

Using her remarkable gifts of penetrating intuition and psychic wisdom, along with countless transformative tools, Kaarin is dedicated to helping people find passion and freedom so they can live consciously empowered. Kaarin can help you make rapid progress toward your heart's deepest desires.

She is the creator of Rabika, a card divination and guidance system for the conscious creator. Receive instant, free online-readings and learn more about Rabika at http://www.rabika.com.

A sought-after speaker, Kaarin also offers tele-seminars and workshops through Rabika University. To learn more about RU classes, go to http://rabika.com/rabika-university.

To schedule an appointment with Kaarin for private sessions go to http://rabika.com/private-sessions-with-kaarin.

Kaarin has also created the Goddess Speak Project to help conscious, entrepreneurial woman bring their wisdom to the world. To learn more about the Goddess Speak Project, go to http://goddess.rabika.com.

Chapter 17

A Recipe in Receiving

How to trust, allow, accept and enjoy what this universe provides

By Maria Kellis

I have discovered that energy play for me is a bit like cooking. I put "ingredients" together in a certain order, stir them all together, toss, bake and a recipe is created. A recipe in receiving is a good recipe to have in your kitchen of magic because no matter how good we are at manifesting if we are not open to receive we cannot hold on to anything we bring into existence. Let's explore this recipe for allowing the abundance of this life and the goodness of this universe to flow towards us. Let us live a life that is full, joyful, easy, free and extraordinary.

Let's start with the ingredients first. Remember in any recipe we start with the freshest and purest ingredients and this is what brings the recipe the flavor that is most palatable. I encourage you to make this recipe your own. Take the ingredients, take the method and once you have practiced a few times, add spice to it and make the flavor be the perfect blend of your own desires.

The first and most important ingredient we are putting together here is trust. Trust is one of those ingredients that is very difficult to find in its purest form, because it is hard to come by. I find that the best way to make trust is to make your own supply of trust, and it is a whole other recipe that I will explain at another time. For now, let me give you the basics of trust, how to recognize trust and how to really have it be a part of you. I can describe how I found trust of the purest form. You cannot ask for trust and receive it, it is the other way around. You trust and this is how you can access this part of life. Trust comes from within and vibrates at a frequency that attracts more trustworthy people, circumstances and events. Trust is simple. It is the absolute certainty that this is a good universe, that this is a good world and that everything that happens is for the highest good for all concerned. So be it. Trust means knowing that everything, absolutely everything, at all times is perfect because it could not be any other way. It is believing despite all evidence to the contrary, that our mind is quick to supply, that this is a good universe and that what we do is for the highest good for all concerned.

Imagine that this realization comes in a vision where we are transported to another time, another space, another reality.

In that dream that may not have been a dream at all if were asked to read the holy texts and understand of the workings of this world, then it would be apparent, just how good this universe really is. We would understand that love is the essence that flows through everything and it is love that permeates all. Not the human brand of love but the love that is unconditional. You can call it divine love if you like that word better. That love is what drives it all together, and the wheel of karma turns in perfect harmony. As the wheel turns, events and circumstances fall in place to accommodate everything in perfect harmony that protects, honors and preserves all. And so it is. Trust is a beautiful ingredient to have always at hand as we go through life because it can really be used in any recipe. Trust is a bit like the salt of this world. The flavor comes out when you add the right amount. A little bit goes a long way.

The second ingredient is gratitude. If trust is the salt then gratitude would be the pepper to use in almost all recipes. Gratitude is an easy enough word to understand and in fact it is an easy ingredient to master and have always available. It is easy because we can start by noticing the little things that we are grateful for. There is no shortage of little things. It can be as simple as noticing that the sun is bright or the plants are beautiful. Nature is an overabundant supply of things we can be grateful for. I like to stop for a second and notice around me 10 things that catch my attention and that make me feel grateful. How fast can I notice them? It is not about wondering if 10 things are there because they certainly are, it is about training that muscle of gratitude so I know how to do it when I need to have gratitude available. Gratitude vibrates in frequencies close to the divine so it is a beautiful ingredient to master. Gratitude will accelerate everything to flow our way. And gratitude will allow us to accept what is coming so the next step follows quickly. Even though spirit does not function in linear time and steps, this reality operates with these rules. So it is beautiful to observe how we can take something non-linear and bring it into linear form and be grateful that it is so.

The next ingredient in the list is the idea of not taking it for granted. It is very much linked to gratitude and yet it brings a slightly different flavor. Whereas gratitude is this deep sense of appreciation for what is and what is to come, not taking it for granted carries the flavor of not taking ourselves and our talents for granted, not comparing ourselves and our talents with others. Knowing that everything we have is uniquely ours to have and to hold and to bring into this world. Because everything that comes through us could only come through us. We have a distinct flavor that we bring into this life, our energy signature so to speak. So we flavor everything we bring into this world with the essence of who we are. There is no competition because we are unique. And there is no race because everything happens on its own divine time. There is nothing to fear because we are always guided and protected. So what is left is to understand that with humility and realize that everything is unique and precious in the same way and appreciating it all in this perfection that it has.

The next ingredient is happiness, joy and laughter. This one is understood by children very well and as we grow older we forget it easily. So it is nice to remember to be like a child as we explore and interact with the world and to bring happiness, laughter and joy into our lives. Every single one of those words is so rich it does it no justice to just throw it in as a simple ingredient yet again laughter is an easy way to start. In Japan they literally would laugh on purpose as an exercise. In other countries of the East they practice laughter yoga. This is becoming a universal realization that the more laughter we have in our lives the more joy we have. Laughter is something that we can do even if it is not coming naturally. Our body does not recognize if we started laughing naturally or if it was a forced laughter. Chemicals and hormones rebalance the same way. And as we laugh then nature takes over and truly laughter brings the secretion of these little hormones that make us feel happy. It is funny to remember that our bodies are simply a collection of matter and energy and chemicals put together and that each and every one of them is useful in its own terms. So go ahead, watch a funny movie, get together with friends and laugh, open up your heart and consciousness to what is and let laughter bring joy and happiness for no reason at all except that they were there to begin with.

The next ingredient again is being excited and it is similar to laughter, joy and happiness and yet it is an ingredient by itself because it implies this sense of anticipation and excitant that we experience when we are children and it is our birthday or it is Christmas and we are about to receive a gift. I remember getting up in the middle of the night to see what Santa Claus was bringing to me because I was so sure that it was going to be coming. I was excited in anticipation and that gave me so much energy. This is the purpose of this ingredient, it acts like a jolt of energy. We can use it as a wonderful thing to have and experience and use that energy that excitement brings into all other areas of our lives as well.

The next ingredient of feeling worthy to receive is a bit tricky to get right, and that is because having self-love and self-acceptance is sometimes conditional. Yet this is the ingredient: feeling worthy to receive. If in our heart we recognize that it is normal to receive and that it is natural then it becomes easier for us to receive. I like to bring humility also into the equation because this is not about believing that we are better (or worse) than anyone else, simply humbly understanding that we are born divine beings and that we have access to all the goodness that the universe has to offer. So when we ask for anything at all, which will instantly start coming our way, maybe we can start for a bit more than what we think is possible so as to build this muscle of receiving. We can always stretch our limits. We can start by what we believe is possible until we know in the deepest parts of our soul and of our being that everything is in fact possible. Then we can ask for what is our dream and then the dream becomes our reality and then we can be so grateful that the whole circle is reinforced and starts again. We can start by knowing, truly knowing, that we are good enough to receive.

Simply realize that it could not be any other way.

Then comes the time for giving up your mind, what I like to call "let go and let God". It is very much a part of trust and yet it is different enough that it is a whole ingredient of its own. It is a beautiful part of any recipe really. I think of it as the time when you put it in the oven and let it bake. Once you have put all the ingredients together you need to give them the right time to act and interact together and this is the part that is a bit tricky to master because it never comes out at our own time, unless we sacrifice a bit of the quality that is. I remember how it was when I was a little kid and we put the cake to bake it in the oven. I wanted to keep opening the door to see how it is doing because the smell was so delicious, so enticing. And then of course this is a good way to prevent the cake from rising. Eventually my mom kindly taught me that I should use the oven light, I am so grateful for the inventor of that light! In our recipe you can always use meditation to help you rise above and observe. It is like the oven light, you can take a peak without disturbing the process. When I was little of course I would sit in front of the oven waiting and waiting. This is part of being a child, everything is so exciting. Maybe then in the beginning we can all sit in front of the oven and play. Now I just put things in the oven and do other things while I am waiting because I know that I put the timer and a little beep will alert me to when the cake is ready, so I can forget about it until the time is right. I have so many other things I want to do. And yes, I do have a confession. Sometimes it is fun to sit in front of the oven and watch the cake rise. So if it is fun by all means enjoy! In life it is even easier. The beep is really finding what you want in front of you and recognizing it as such, and that is acceptance.

Acceptance comes last and it is like the part of tasting the food. Yet in the order of this recipe it does come rather at the end. Accept and trust, yes here is trust again, that what was given is what we could have at this point in time in our lives, in our existence. I have realized over the years and countless experiments that even though our soul or spirit or higher self is absolutely perfect just the way it is, there is a counterpart of a physical existence that is always striving to become as such, to resonate at the same frequency that is. And our mind, this judge that is our mind, is always finding something wrong with the physical existence part because of some reason, of some smudge, of some misalignment of the perfect idea that we hold in our mind. Except we forget that our mind is not perfect, it is only a part of the physical existence so whatever it conceives is only as good as the physical existence. If then we accept what is as part of the divine plan for us, and yes indeed that is part of the trust always, then there is no misalignment to be called for. Because what came is what we needed at that time, at that place, taking into account all the circumstances of that moment. This is what could fit with us at that time. So then we allow it to come by accepting the perfection of what is and this is what will bring more into existence. Because the rest of our desire is on its way in the same way that the first part of it came to us. It just will come to us on its own time again. And what is even more difficult to accept is that if we do not accept what is, we act as if we are closing the door to the rest of what is to come from coming our way.

So let us put together trust, gratitude, not taking it for granted, happiness, joy, laughter and excitement, let us feel worthy to receive, let go and let God and accept. I hope that you enjoy receiving in your life al that this coming your way. There is an abundance in this universe that we can truly believe in. This abundance is extraordinary because there is no effort to create anything. It is our heart that calls anything into existence and every heartbeat is a beacon for everything and anything to come. When we trust in our hearts that this is a good universe and that this is a good experience and it really could not be any other way because it is so, then we can truly experience what is good continuously. In a funny way we already are. Let us truly and freely experience life with ease, grace and joy, let us always allow happiness to flow our way. May it be so. SO BE IT!

I would encourage you to try this recipe. See how it works for you, add your own ingredients and flavors and if you want to share your improvement on this recipe please contact me at maria.kellis@gmail.com and share your feedback and comments with me. This is a collective game of consciousness that we are playing and when we all together share what is then we all together grow and evolve.

ABOUT THE AUTHOR: *MARIA KELLIS*

Rev. Maria Kellis is a certified spiritual healer. She has been helping people find out how to strengthen their desires and make their dreams come true. After many accidents, pain and a near death experience, from being a business person and an engineer, she has totally switched gears – she now shares the joy of life - she travels around the world – and she works as a coach for people to connect to their purposes. These days her home base is Bali, Indonesia. She has managed to restore her health, achieved independence and lives a life of freedom.

For all these, she has found a way to achieve effortlessly and enjoyably while still performing in this world at the highest levels. Generating miracles is the answer to life's problems. Money, fame, health, and relationships: The question is not if you can do it, rather how fast can you do it?

Maria Kellis was born In Greece, grew up in France, and went to college in the United States. She holds two degrees from MIT, a degree from the Sloan School of Management and a degree from the Academie of Cannes. She has achieved high honors and high level positions. She achieved a lot in her life as a person of this world. She worked hard and participated in the creation of companies. She was able to get also great jobs – as high as working as an advisor to the Vice President of Greece, and as head of the technical services for the Church of Greece.

Chapter 18

Shine Your Light, Know your Gifts

By Erica Glessing

I have these memories when I was two years old, and we lived in the gorgeous town of Sausalito, California. We lived in a home that overlooked the ocean, and I was a bright and shiny being. I loved to open the door and greet visitors. I loved to make people feel at home.

That child left and a young uncertain girl in teens became uncomfortable with her gifts. I didn't like to shine so bright! I was always singled out by my teachers to show off how well I could learn. I was always asked to read out loud or speak in front of the classroom. I became uncomfortable in my body, and I stopped liking myself. I didn't like my curves, my womanly fullness that showed up around age 12.

A few things happened to dim my light and I chose to marry

someone who couldn't understand my gifts at all. Over 20 years of hard and difficult living took a toll. I stopped expressing my light. I chose to accept all the wrongness and heaviness of me. I chose to accept that it was wrong to be curvy and wrong to be full of me. I went into a darkness that did not break until I hit my 50s.

As I step now into the greatness of receiving my gifts, I feel the light pour through from my being each day. It's funny when you have breakthroughs and people look at you like it was easy. They don't see the years of horror that preceeded the shiny light that you can be. Perhaps you will now reach for your own light more quickly knowing how long I waited to reach for mine!

Here are some of the ways I became clear on my own gifted nature, my own light shining so brightly and asking so loudly to come out and play with other great bringers of light.

- Each day, create a practice of activities and opportunities that will expand your light.

- Know that your "regular" operating mind will argue against change. Be prepared to shock yourself when you are waking up your light - change doesn't happen without change. I mean, if you are living here, and you want to live there, you can't keep living here.

- Then, when you ask, be prepared to leap into the answers.

For the new way of being is calling you, and this is a tug on your spirit. This is a calling that might feel like you "should" be bigger about you, or know yourself more, or write a novel, or speak in front of people. You might resonate with Tony Robbins or you might resonate with Marci Shimoff. And then you think how can I think I am like that? I am reminded of the newer rendition of the movie "Dr. Doolittle" where Eddie Murphy is told "You are a doctor who can talk to animals, that is who you are." Perhaps, you are a light worker, and it is time to shine your light, and that is who you are.

I've learned so much bringing this book into your hands. As the bringer of this book, I visioned written pieces that would open us all up to our own greatness, to see the very nature of our own being as precious and beautiful.

I am stunned by the stories and gifts that came from the writers of this book. I'm going to call out the work of Ken Elliott on manifestation, because the reading of his chapter worked on me in a way that I would like to share with you all.

I saw in reading Ken's chapter the way that dreams come to us, and the how, and the meaning, and the greatness of our dreams. And I'm not talking about what happens when you are sleeping. I'm talking about that big huge amazing dream you have inside of you – to be something, to become something, to stand in the light of something, to stand up for something, to change something, to right a wrong, to bring healing, whatever that dream be.

I would ask you in this moment, to move into your dream

just a few more inches. Move a little closer to your dream. Here is what I was shown about your dreams and why they show up.

When you have a dream, you are inviting a new reality to unfold. You may have been slapped or slammed down for having wild big crazy hairy loving yummy exciting extraterrestrial dreams. What happened when you dreamed, when you were young? What happened to those dreams? Are you willing to wake up to your dreams again now?

For all of life is changing. All of reality is shifting. Your dreams are so much closer now than they have ever been in history, and your ability to change the future has changed forever. Your dreams become reality more quickly now than any other time in history. Reality begins to formulate as you dream, and it becomes more and more palpable, and this is an absolute.

In one practical example, let's talk about Twitter. Let's talk about the power of Twitter to bring you right up in the face of some of the most famous people in the world. So let's say you would like to write songs. Write a song, put it on a website, link the website of your song to someone who gives you awe. What if they love it? What if they reach out and remember when they were starting out and someone gave them a hand? You are just inches away from the people who were once impossible to reach. What kind of power is that light of you to now connect with others?

Begin to create your dreams with a new sense of awe and appreciation for your own gifts.

Here is another insight - what if you don't ask? Nothing can happen if you don't ask. I woke up a few weeks ago and realized that it was time to own a car. My car had been taken out by a woman who drove into it (no one was hurt) and I was using a rental car for a few months. I woke up one day and said "it's time," and a few hours later, I owned a new car. I had been in paralysis because I wasn't clear what kind of car I wanted, nor how much car I wanted to afford. When I shifted and asked for insight for "the perfect car," whatever that is - not with the full knowledge of the right car, but just the ask, the perfect car with three rows of seating for my kids (yes the car seats eight, I have three kids who sometimes like to bring a friend) and great mileage and it's even green (my favorite color for cars) and so it is. The right car just walked in and gave itself to me, search complete. It took only a few hours to get the car, but it took the click into "today is the right day for me to own a car again," feeling to shift that into reality.

What else is possible that you have not asked for yet? What dream have you carried around, afraid to ask for it to become reality? Are you willing to ask louder for your dream today?

I saw clearly in my mind's eye that dreams begin to become real far before they are real in your reality. That is, by asking the dream to be in your life, the dream begins to form. Then, the opportunities begin to show up that fit that picture in your life.

Here is another example that happened for me a month or so ago. I was dreaming about my books on happiness being written with full color images to inspire people on each page. I write original "Happiness Quotations," and I was seeing a book published in full color, but I hadn't gotten to clarity on how I would find all of the color images to illustrate the book. I wasn't sure if I would work with a lot of photographers, or pull photos from photo banks on the web, or how I would approach this. One morning I woke up and sketched out a page, how I wanted the full color image to show up right next to my words.

Later that day I saw a photographer emerge on Twitter whose work was stunning. I approached him and asked him if he was interested in publishing his own book. He said "call me sometime," and I picked up that phone That Very Instant and called him. I said "Hi, this is Erica," and he said "Who?" I said "You said call me sometime, I thought this would be a good time." His name is Richard Cruse, and you will love our new books. The first book is called "Happiness Quotations: for days when the rainbows are hiding," and it will be released later this spring. It's stunning with his photos and it is inspirational with the quotations I keep writing each day. So what magic is possible for you if you would be willing to see it?

Please stop now and write down some dream you have had

that you gave up on, or invite a new dream to show up. Ask yourself what is your dream? Could you live it? Could you live it bigger?

Know that your dreams show up for a reason, and in receiving your dream, you are receiving your gift. You were not born to be miserable, of this I am certain.

Stand in the light of the dream you hold and know that your gifts would love to be bigger on this planet at this time. Your gifts are asking to shine, so be that light you truly be.

Ask for more, again, and then ask for more, again, and then once that's good, ask for more, again. Know that you can't possibly know all that is possible for new possibilities are being formed each day. New opportunities are showing up, each day. New dreams are being born. New cars are being built. New technologies are being discovered. So every time someone makes up a new reality, your dream can change. This awakening is part of the human spirit in triumph, and you are so blessed to be alive right now during this time of major transformation into the light.

Let us join hands in spirit, and be true to our dreams.

ABOUT THE AUTHOR: *Erica Glessing*

Erica Glessing is a dreamer, a bright writer, an editor, a publisher, a medium, an animal communicator, a mom, a happiness coach, and a loving spirit.

You can find out more about Erica at www.EricaGlessing.com, www.happycoaching.biz, www.Facebook.com/happinessquotations, www.HappinessQuotations.com, www.HappinessTelesummit.com, and feel free to friend her on Facebook or follow her on Twitter.

Her company, Happy Publishing, is dedicated to publishing the works of light bringers on the planet.

The END

About Happy Publishing

Happy Publishing is dedicated to supporting authors who wish to change the world. Happy Publishing has published more than 125 authors since its inception. Books released so far include:

Manifest Change

The Dreams of Mattie Fitch

Something About Sophia

The Energy of Happiness

Happiness Quotations

Luxury Home Selling Mastery

Home Buying Mastery

Sell Your House Fast for the Right Price!

Coming in 2015:

The Energy of Expansion (March, 2015)

The Energy of Healing (April, 2015)

The Energy of Creativity (May, 2015)

And what else is possible?

Erica Glessing is the CEO of Happy Publishing. Happy Publishing is under Ingram, the finest book distribution company on the planet today.

Erica is a third generation publisher, and second generation published author. She began writing professionally in 1984 as a news reporter. She wrote *Prospect When You Are Happy,* in 2007; and *Happiness Quotations: Gentle Reminders of Your Preciousness,* in 2011.

She works with writers to bring out the best in them. Happy Publishing was formed with the writer in mind.

Email HappyPublishing@gmail.com.

Happy Publishing

CPSIA information can be obtained at www.ICGtesting.com
Printed in the USA
LVOW04s0705080315

429586LV00003B/25/P

9 780989 555494